ESTHER
AND THE
COVENANT WAR

AN EXPOSITORY STUDY

ESTHER
AND THE
COVENANT WAR

*AN EXPOSITORY STUDY OF
THE BOOK OF ESTHER*

TABITHA MIN

RITTER HOUSE
PUBLISHING

www.tabithamin.com

Book and Cover design by Tabitha Min

ISBN: 979-8-9877812-9-6

First Edition: November 2025

10 9 8 7 6 5 4 3 2 1

For all the ladies in Bible study, thank you for trusting me with this journey through Esther and for your incredible support, faith, and insight week after week.

And to my dear friend Beth, thank you for walking beside me in my hour of need and for encouraging me to step out in faith. Your friendship has been a reflection of God's grace and strength in my life.

TABLE OF CONTENTS

ACKNOWLEDGEMENTS

First and foremost, I give all glory and thanks to God, whose faithfulness has been the anchor of this study and the author of every revelation within it. His Word continues to prove living and active, shaping not only what is written here but the heart behind it.

To my family, thank you for your patience, encouragement, and love through countless late nights of writing, teaching, and revising. You have been my constant reminder of grace and purpose.

To my church family and Bible study sisters, your hunger for truth and your willingness to wrestle with Scripture have breathed life into these pages. Each of you has helped turn a series of notes into a living testimony of God's covenant faith-fulness.

Finally, to everyone who will read and study these words, thank you for joining me in this journey through Esther. May you see in her story the same victorious thread that runs from Eden's promise to the cross of Christ, and may it remind you that God is still waging and winning His covenant war through us today.

PREFACE

This book began, quite simply, as a weekly Bible study.

A small group of wonderful women with a deep desire to know Scripture more fully asked me to lead a study through the book of Esther. Week by week, we gathered with our Bibles open, diving deep into the text, sometimes pausing over a single verse, sometimes tracing its connections across the whole of Scripture. Those sessions shaped much of what you now hold in your hands.

I am not a scholar, nor do I have formal theological training. I am simply someone who loves Scripture, deeply and often imperfectly. What was once a critical, analytical nature in me, the Lord has redeemed as His love language. Study has become worship for me and research has become relationship. And the Word, always alive, continues to meet me in ways that leave me in awe of its Author.

As a writer of fantasy and fiction, I have always loved storytelling. But what I find most breathtaking is the supernatural narrative of Scripture itself and the masterclass of literary design that transcends all human ability. The way its themes, symbols, and typology weave seamlessly across generations is nothing short of miraculous. Whether you zoom in to a single verse or step back to see the panorama of redemption, every thread forms part of an intricate tapestry that reveals Christ at the center.

My hope is that as you read this study, your own passion for Scripture will be rekindled. May you find yourself caught up in its living cadence and drawn deeper into the same wonder that captivated our group each week. The Word of God is alive and breathing, and it calls to each of us to wade deeper into its living waters.

May this study be an invitation to see His hand where He seems hidden, to hear His voice in the silence, and to discover that the story of Esther, like every part of Scripture, speaks the name of Jesus from beginning to end.

INTRODUCTION

The story of Esther is often told as a tale of bravery within a Persian palace about a young woman who rose from obscurity to save her people. But beneath that familiar story lies something far older and far greater: the continuation of God's covenant war and how the war that began in Eden, carried on through the wilderness battles of Israel, and culminated at the Cross of Christ.

This study exists to reveal Esther not as an isolated account of courage, but as a vital link in the chain of God's redemptive plan. What happened in Persia was part of the same spiritual conflict that began with the serpent's deception in Genesis and found its victory at Golgotha.

Through the pages of Esther, we see the clash between two seeds; the seed of promise and the seed of opposition, played out in royal courts and human hearts. My hope is that as you journey through this study, you will not only see how God fought for His covenant people then, but recognize how He is still waging that same war in and through His people today.

This book follows the structure of the biblical text itself, covering one chapter of Esther per week as it blends scriptural exposition, historical background, and practical reflection. Each lesson unfolds the story's layers of meaning while pointing to the ultimate revelation of Christ's covenant victory.

While God's name is never explicitly mentioned in the book of Esther, His presence saturates every moment of the narrative. That hiddenness is the very heart of the study as we learn to recognize the unseen hand of God in the midst of spiritual warfare, divine timing, and human decisions.

When I first began teaching the book of Esther, I didn't realize how profoundly its message would mirror my own walk with God. What began as a simple chapter study for our women's Bible group became a revelation of God's covenant faithfulness, not just to Israel, but to every believer called to stand in their appointed time.

As the weeks unfolded, we discovered together that Esther's story wasn't just history, it was still speaking into our lives today. The insights and discussions from that study shaped this book, and I'm deeply grateful for the women who walked this journey beside me and helped give it a living voice.

You are not just reading about a queen's courage; you are stepping into a covenant story that spans creation to the cross, and beyond. Whether your obedience looks like Esther's quiet faith or Mordecai's bold defiance, you stand in the same cosmic narrative of victory and redemption.

As you turn these pages, may your eyes open to see the invisible war, your heart anchor in God's sovereignty, and your spirit rise in the confidence that He still reigns in every generation of His people.

Welcome to the covenant war.

CHAPTER ONE

The Banquet and the Hidden Hand of God

In those days, the palace where King Ahasuerus sat on the royal throne of his kingdom was in Susa. ~Esther 1:2

A Nation in Exile

The book of Esther opens not in Jerusalem, but in exile. God's people live scattered and dispersed throughout the vast reaches of a foreign empire. There is no temple, no prophet, no altar of worship rising in prayer. And most striking of all, there is no direct mention of God anywhere in its pages.

Yet this silence is not absence. The omission itself becomes the author's most brilliant revelation in which it invites the reader to discern God's sovereignty working behind the veil of history.

While the narrative unfolds amid the grandeur of Persia, God's unseen governance directs every turn. What seems to be a tale of politics and pride is, in truth, the stage upon which God's providence moves in secret.

King Ahasuerus—known historically as Xerxes I—rules over an empire stretching from India to Ethiopia, 127 provinces in all. The opening verse situates us in a world of spectacle and ambition, where human strength appears absolute. Xerxes, intoxicated by his own power, hosts a lavish 180-day feast for his officials, followed by a seven-day royal banquet in his capital, Susa.

These feasts were more than indulgence; they were political theater, and acts of propaganda designed to secure loyalty and project invincibility. History tells us these events likely coincided with his campaign against Greece, the same war remembered through the legend of Leonidas and the 300 at Thermopylae.

But the irony is poignant. While Ahasuerus gathers his nobles to prepare for conquest, heaven is already preparing for deliverance. The empire may flaunt its strength, but God is setting the stage for reversal. And what man builds through arrogance, God will overturn through humility.

The Wine-Soaked Court

The Persian court was a kingdom of excess. Ancient historians describe a culture where wine flowed as freely as power. The Greeks wrote that Persian councils were often held under the influence of drink, believing that intoxication freed the mind to speak truth and commune with the divine.

For King Xerxes, this intoxication became a test of loyalty, and a way to expose who would bend and who would break under his rule. But Scripture presents a sharper contrast.

Human rulers sought revelation through indulgence while God reveals His wisdom through hiddenness.

The empire's pursuit of clarity through pleasure only deepens its blindness. For while Persia seeks truth in the haze of excess, heaven is quietly unveiling purpose through restraint.

Even the mightiest empire, swollen with wealth and self-confidence, cannot outmaneuver the sovereignty of God. What seems like human control is, in truth, God's hand of orchestration.

The first chapter thus establishes a spiritual contrast that sets the tone for the entire chapter:

- Man uses wine to uncover truth.
- God uses hiddenness to unveil His plan.

So, the stage is now set: a kingdom intoxicated with its own grandeur, a ruler blinded by pride, and a silent God whose invisible hand is already weaving redemption through the folly of men.

The Queen's Refusal

"Also, Vashti the queen made a feast for the women in the royal house which belonged to King Ahasuerus." ~Esther 1:9

As the men feast in the king's court, Queen Vashti hosts her own banquet for the women of the palace. Yet her story will soon ignite the first spark of movement for this narrative. When Xerxes, drunk with pride and desire for display, summons Vashti to appear before his guests and parade her beauty, she refuses.

Her defiance shatters the illusion of control. What begins as a domestic scene of royal indulgence becomes a crisis that shakes the empire. One woman's refusal exposes the fragility of worldly power, and the same empire that can subdue nations cannot command the heart of one queen.

The author uses this moment to expose the hollow nature of earthly authority. The world's mightiest ruler cannot govern his own household. The spectacle of strength collapses under the weight of pride.

Yet even this act of resistance serves a hidden purpose in which God is at work within the cracks of human pride, using disobedience to open the door for deliverance.

When Vashti refuses the king, she unknowingly creates the vacancy that God's providence intends to fill. Her dismissal becomes the first step in a redemptive sequence that will soon raise up a young Jewish woman—Esther—whose obedience will save her people.

The Beginning

Thus, the book opens not with the grandeur of spiritual revelation, but with the unfolding of irony. The story begins in a palace that knows only excess, under a ruler who mistakes indulgence for authority. And yet, through that same empire's folly, God begins His work of salvation.

Esther 1 reminds us that even when God's name is unspoken, His will is unhindered. His sovereignty is not diminished by silence, but that it is displayed through it. The feast of Persia becomes the prelude to the fast of faith, and the absence of God's voice becomes the invitation to look for His hand.

CHAPTER ONE

Two Women, Two Realms

Esther 1 introduces a tension that reveals a unique contrast between two women, two refusals, and two realms.

- Vashti refuses the king's summons; Esther risks her life to approach him.
- Vashti is cast out; Esther is raised up.
- Vashti exposes the pride of man; Esther exposes the plot of the enemy.
- Vashti destabilizes an empire; Esther delivers a nation.

The story of Vashti's fall and Esther's rise forms more than a narrative transition, it creates a theological mirror. Through it, we glimpse the pattern of reversal by the God who dethrones one to raise another, and who humbles the proud to exalt the obedient.

Vashti's refusal, though born of dignity, exposes the moral rot beneath Persian luxury. Her "no" becomes a mirror reflecting the emptiness of power that objectifies and consumes. Yet Esther's story enters precisely where Vashti's ends. Vashti resisted humiliation; Esther risked her life for salvation. Both display courage, but of different kinds: one is self-preserving, while the other self-giving.

When Vashti stood for herself, Esther would stand for her people. And through both, God exposes pride and magnifies humility, proving that even acts outside the covenant can still serve His sovereign purpose.

This literary symmetry—known as *chiastic design*—presents the story like an hourglass. What begins with pride descends into reversal, and then ascends again through obedience. The God who "hides" Himself in this book is not absent; He is the invisible architect, weaving redemption through paradox.

So, the first queen's fall is a human drama of politics and pride, whereas the second queen's rise is a spiritual drama of providence and purpose. Together they form a single truth that ripples through Scripture: *"He has brought down the mighty from their thrones and exalted those of humble estate." ~Luke 1:52*

In this contrast, the reader is prepared for the theme that defines the entire book, and indeed the entire Bible in which God overturns the mighty and exalts the humble.

Literary and Theological Reflection

Though the name of God never appears in *Esther*, His fingerprints mark every moment. The silence is deliberate. It trains the reader to look closer and to perceive God's presence beneath human events.

Through the lens of faith, what seems ordinary becomes extraordinary. A royal banquet becomes a spiritual appointment. A queen's refusal becomes the opening act of redemption. And a pagan empire becomes the instrument of covenant preservation.

Thus, the book becomes a masterclass in hidden providence in how God governs the visible world through invisible power.

Two realities unfold in parallel:

- The physical realm of feasts, decrees, and royal intrigue.
- The spiritual realm of orchestration, preservation, and spiritual warfare.

Those who read only the surface will find a moral story about courage and coincidence. But those who look deeper will recognize the covenant war still unfolding through a continuation of the conflict first declared in Eden, between the seed of promise and the seed of opposition.

In the palace of Susa, as in the garden of Eden, the battle between pride and promise begins again. But where man hides God's name, God hides His plan and still brings it to completion.

Modern Parallels and the Connection to Christ

The pattern of reversal introduced in Esther 1 is not confined to Persia. It repeats through every age, revealing a repeating pattern woven into the fabric of redemption itself. Vashti and Esther stand as portraits of two kingdoms at war, two spirits in conflict, and two ways by which God reveals His glory.

Their contrast mirrors the great tension that has existed since Eden:

- The Flesh vs. The Spirit

  "If you live according to the flesh, you will die; but if by the Spirit you put to death the deeds of the body, you will live." ~Romans 8:13

  Vashti represents human dignity resisting corruption and the flesh refusing to be degraded. Esther represents spiritual surrender fulfilling redemption by the spirit yielding to God's purpose. One resists humiliation; the other risks everything for restoration. Both are used by God to expose pride and exalt purpose, revealing that even in op-position, His hand governs the outcome.

- Pride vs. Providence
  "I will get glory over Pharaoh and all his host." ~Exodus 14:17–18

  "For My own sake, for My own sake, I do it... My glory I will not give to another." ~Isaiah 48:11

  "For Your name's sake You lead me and guide me." ~Psalm 31:3

  "Yet He saved them for His name's sake, that He might make His mighty power known." ~Psalm 106:8

Throughout Scripture, God allows pride to ascend only so that He might reveal its collapse. Human ambition rises like a tower, and heaven waits until the moment it topples under its own weight. Then, through the wreckage, the wisdom of God emerges.

So it is in Esther. What begins as chaos—a drunken feast, a dismissed queen, and a volatile empire—is in truth a prelude to redemption. Every misstep of man becomes a stepping stone in the unfolding plan of God.

Even when He seems absent, His purposes move with precision, and every moment of disorder is quietly aligned with His order. The silence of chapter one is not God's neglect, it is His strategy. God is already writing deliverance into the backdrop of exile, turning what appears meaningless into the first movement of a redemptive symphony that will culminate in the cross.

For in Christ, this same pattern finds its completion: the humble are exalted, the proud are brought low, and God's hand is revealed through suffering. So, the reversals of Esther are the echoes of Calvary.

CLOSING REMARKS

The opening chapter of Esther reveals a simple truth in that God's providence has already accounted for our imperfection. His sovereignty does not tremble beneath our failures.

As one might otherwise put it, "God has already factored our stupidity into His plan." The point is not irreverence, but reassurance. His will is not fragile. Our missteps do not derail His design, as they often become the very means through which His purposes unfold.

So, Vashti's refusal, Xerxes' pride, and Persia's confusion all serve the ultimate unfolding of God's preparation. The book begins in exile and silence, but God is already setting the board for reversal. And when the throne rooms of men rage with pride and fear, the throne of heaven remains unmoved.

This first chapter closes not with resolution, but with anticipation. The feasts of Persia will soon give way to the fasts of faith, and the stage is set for the deliverance of a covenant people.

CHAPTER ONE

REFLECTION & DISCUSSION

1. Silence is never the same as absence. God often hides His hand not to distance Himself, but to deepen our discernment, inviting us to trust that His sovereignty is at work even when His voice cannot be heard.

   Where might God be moving quietly in your own life, asking you to believe He is present even when He seems hidden?

2. Vashti's defiance preserved her dignity, while Esther's obedience preserved her people. Both stood firm, yet in opposite ways; one by refusal, the other by surrender.

   How do you discern when God is calling you to resist what is wrong versus yield in faith to what feels impossible?

3. Every generation builds its own Persia. The idols of power, beauty, and control still rule cultural empires that measure worth by appearance and dominance rather than by holiness and humility.

   Where might you be tempted to conform to these values, and how is God inviting you to live set apart within your own modern empire?

4. God's presence often hides in plain sight. He weaves the miraculous through the mundane, and His timing through what feels like delay.

   How might recognizing that partnership between the natural and the spiritual reshape the way you respond to waiting, detours, or disappointment?

5. The story opens with a feast of pride but ends with a whisper of redemption. What begins as chaos is already under construction for reversal, because in God's hands, even disorder becomes design.

   Where in your life might present confusion, loss, or uncertainty actually be preparing the groundwork for His hidden redemption?

CHAPTER TWO

Esther's Rise

After these things, when the wrath of King Ahasuerus had subsided, he remembered Vashti... ~Esther 2:1

The scene opens in the aftermath of pride's downfall. And the empire that once roared with celebration now sits in uneasy silence. The great king of Persia, once intoxicated with his own grandeur, now sobers beneath the weight of his own decree. His anger has cooled, but the consequences remain. The permanence of his law becomes the mirror of his impotence, and an empire bound not by wisdom, but by its own vanity.

Xerxes' Regret and the Counsel of Men

"Then the king's servants who attended him said: "Let beautiful young virgins be sought for the king..." ~Esther 2:2

When the wrath of Ahasuerus subsides, the text records that "he remembered Vashti." This is not repentance but nostalgia, and a memory stained with the regret that follows unrestrained pride. Yet because his word is law, even remorse cannot reverse what his ego has decreed.

Here, the weakness of the Persian throne is exposed. Its strength lies in image, not integrity, and in proclamation, not principle. And unable to face his own failure, the king turns not to humility, but to counsel. The voices around him offer no wisdom, only distraction. Their solution to his emptiness is indulgence: replace conviction with comfort, and remorse with pleasure.

So, they propose a search for the most beautiful virgins in the land, a parade of appearance meant to conceal a kingdom's insecurity. This is humanity's oldest reflex, to cover shame with spectacle, and to seek meaning in what can be displayed rather than in what must be transformed.

Vashti's refusal had exposed the empire's fragility. So, the officials' solution now seeks to hide that fragility beneath beauty. Yet even in this shallow pursuit, God is preparing a deliverer for His people.

The stage is quietly being set for the arrival of a young Jewish woman whose humility will outshine every crown in the court.

And what the world calls coincidence, Scripture calls providence.

Xerxes Leaves for War

Between verses 4 and 8 lies a gap in the biblical timeline that is filled by history. Greek and Persian records tell us that Xerxes departed for war against Greece soon after issuing this decree. He returned a year later in defeat with his armies crushed and his pride shattered.

The humbled king who could not conquer Greece will soon be conquered by grace. And his military failure becomes the soil from which God's redemptive favor will sprout.

Before Esther even enters the palace, God is already dismantling the arrogance of men who believe themselves in-vincible. Just as Pharaoh's heart was hardened to display God's power, Xerxes' pride is broken to make room for God's plan.

The Gathering of Women

"So it was, when the king's command and decree were heard, and when many young women were gathered at Shushan the citadel..." ~Esther 2:8

In the king's absence, his decree is carried out with imperial efficiency. Across the empire, young women are taken from their homes and gathered, not by choice, but by command. What appears to the world as an opportunity is, in truth, an act of possession. This was not a royal beauty contest but a royal conscription. Each woman was brought to the citadel and placed under the custody of Hegai, the eunuch in charge of the harem; a gilded prison masked in luxury.

They were to undergo twelve months of preparation:

Six months in oil of myrrh — for cleansing, healing, and softening.

Six months in perfumes and spices — for fragrance, allure, and ritual refinement.

But beneath the political surface lies a spiritual pattern: God often prepares His vessels through long seasons of hidden refinement. Before Esther could stand before a king, she had to learn to dwell in waiting.

The Introduction of Mordecai and Esther

"In Shushan the citadel there was a certain Jew whose name was Mordecai..." ~Esther 2:5

The narrative now shifts from the grandeur of the palace to the streets of the people, and from the stage of kings to the simplicity of a home.

In the capital of Shushan (Susa) lives a man named Mordecai, introduced not through titles or achievements, but through lineage; "the son of Jair, the son of Shimei, the son of Kish, a Benjamite." This detail is deliberate. By tracing his ancestry back to Kish, the author draws a direct line to King Saul, Israel's first monarch, who centuries earlier failed to destroy Agag, the king of the Amalekites (1 Samuel 15). That unfinished act of disobedience now reverberates through the generations, setting the stage for a new confrontation between the descendants of Saul and Agag, and between Mordecai and Haman.

Mordecai lives in exile, under pagan rule, yet remains steadfast in loyalty to God's people. He embodies the faith that does not depend on signs, and the kind that endures without visible favor.

Beside him stands his young cousin Hadassah, called Esther, whom he has raised as his own daughter after the death of her parents. Her name itself tells the story: Hadassah (meaning "myrtle") evokes fragrance and life; Esther (from the Persian "star," or possibly from the Hebrew root Hester, meaning "hidden") foreshadows the providential concealment at the heart of this entire book.

Her beginnings which are marked by loss, obscurity, and exile become the very soil in which God's plan of reversal will bloom. From a humble home in a foreign city, God begins to weave a redemptive thread that will one day unravel an empire's decree.

Esther Enters the Palace

"So it was, when the king's command and decree were heard... Esther also was taken to the king's palace."
~Esther 2:8–9

The girl of obscurity is suddenly thrust into the glittering heart of an empire. Taken into the king's court under the custody of Hegai, the eunuch charged with overseeing the women, Esther finds herself surrounded by opulence, ritual, and competition. Yet even here, her quiet dignity distinguishes her.

The text notes that she "found favor" in Hegai's eyes — a recurring theme throughout Esther's story. This favor is not a product of charm or manipulation; it is the silent current of grace that flows through her life. Esther is not striving for position, she is simply walking in providence.

And Hegai, perceiving something uncommon in her spirit, grants her special privileges: preferred treatment, chosen provisions, and seven maidens from the palace. So, what appears to be administrative courtesy becomes supernatural orchestration, and a reflection of how God positions His chosen even within the structures of men.

The Seven Maidservants

The number seven is also no incidental detail. In Persian culture, it represented completeness and royal honor. Xerxes himself surrounded his throne with seven nobles of counsel (Esther 1:14), the highest circle of authority in his court. But in Scripture, seven carries a deeper meaning. It speaks of God's order and covenant fullness:

- Seven days of creation (Genesis 1)
- The seven-branched lampstand (Exodus 25:37)
- The sevenfold Spirit of God (Isaiah 11:2; Revelation 1:4)

Thus, what appears to be an earthly arrangement becomes a spiritual symbol. Esther is surrounded by seven maidservants; a quiet sign that she lacks nothing needed for her calling. So, what the world assigns by rank, God redeems by purpose.

Xerxes' seven princes of power symbolize the might of man, but Esther's seven maidens of service symbolize the sufficiency of God.

Through this contrast, the text reveals another truth:

God's kingdom does not mirror the hierarchies of men.

Where human empires exalt domination, God honors devotion. Where the world prizes strength, He magnifies servanthood. Even in the most unlikely of settings — a pagan palace — God surrounds His chosen vessel with the fullness of provision.

Esther Conceals Her Identity

"Esther had not revealed her people or her family, for Mordecai had charged her not to make it known." ~Esther 2:10

In obedience to Mordecai's instruction, Esther conceals her identity. But her silence is not deception; it is discernment. What God hides, He hides with purpose. Just as His own name remains unspoken throughout the book, so Esther's heritage remains concealed as this revelation will be revealed in its appointed time.

So, this concealment becomes a central motif in the theology of Esther in which God's hand works invisibly before His glory is revealed openly. And his servants often remain hidden in plain sight, prepared for a moment that has not yet arrived.

She does not yet know that her obedience in concealment is as crucial as her boldness will later be in revelation. But through both, God is teaching her — and us — that faith sometimes waits as quietly as it acts.

So before deliverance is declared, it must first be disguised.

Mordecai at the Gate

"And every day Mordecai walked before the court of the women's quarters, to learn of Esther's welfare and what was happening to her". ~Esther 2:11

Each day, Mordecai passes by the gate of the women's court, quietly waiting for word of Esther's welfare. What seems like the

simple act of a guardian's concern is far more than paternal instinct, it is prophetic positioning.

Throughout Scripture, the gate represents more than a physical entryway; it is a spiritual threshold. It is where justice is rendered, counsel is given, and destiny turns its hinges:

- The seat of justice (Ruth 4:1) — where redemption was
declared.
- The place of counsel and intercession (Proverbs 31:23) —
where wisdom and advocacy meet.
- The threshold of reversal (Esther 6:10–12) — where Mordecai
himself will later be exalted.

Thus, Mordecai's presence at the gate foreshadows his future
role as an intercessor and deliverer. He is standing on the literal
threshold between exile and redemption. And his faithfulness in
waiting mirrors the patience of heaven itself, which often lingers at
the threshold of human decision, guiding history without spectacle.

Esther's True Favor

*"She asked for nothing except what Hegai, the king's eunuch,
advised..." ~Esther 2:15*

When Esther's turn comes to stand before the king, her response is markedly different from the others. While many likely
grasped for what might enhance their appearance or favor, Esther
asks for nothing beyond what is advised.

Her restraint reveals a deep trust, not in appearance or chance, but in providence. She listens more than she demands, and she yields rather than strives. This is not passivity but discernment, the wisdom to know that favor flows from alignment, not ambition.

Through this, her grace moves in two directions:

- Outwardly, she carries beauty that draws the eye.
- Inwardly, she carries meekness that draws the heart.

The text tells us that she found favor with all who saw her, and ultimately, with the king himself. But in the spiritual realm, a greater exchange is taking place. The orphan becomes queen, and the exile becomes chosen. The vessel of deliverance steps quietly into her appointed role even as she fails to see it thus far. So, the reversal begins not through miracle or might, but through favor, obedience, and timing.

Theological Reflection

From the opening chapter to this moment, Esther's rise has been anything but accidental. Every detail from her orphanhood, her exile, the king's regret, the beauty regimen, and the seven maidens, is a thread in the tapestry of God's masterful design. Where the world sees coincidence, faith sees coordination.

This entire chapter rests upon a dual reality in which worldly ambition seeks control, and God's providence seeks positioning. So, the empire's search for beauty is simultaneously God's search for obedience. And the very system built to glorify itself becomes the stage for God's salvation.

God often hides His deliverer within the machinery of oppression, the same way He would one day hide redemption within a manger, and victory within a cross.

Esther's Character

"So, Esther was taken to King Ahasuerus into his royal house... and the king loved Esther above all the women." ~Esther 2:16–17

The narrative now shifts from preparation to coronation. Esther, the girl who once lived in obscurity, is crowned queen of the Persian Empire. Yet Scripture draws our eyes away from the spectacle of the crown and toward the posture of her heart.

Her rise is not marked by ambition or manipulation. It is marked by meekness; a rare and radiant strength that neither strives nor resists, but yields to God's shaping. Esther listens more than she speaks; she observes before she acts, and she trusts before she understands.

In a world defined by self-assertion, her restraint becomes her greatest strength. Meekness is not weakness, it is power under control. So, Esther's composure is her weapon. She acts with conviction, yet only when the time is right.

This is true wisdom; the kind that does not force outcomes but waits for God's appointed moment. The kind of wisdom that would later be seen in Christ's own ministry, where silence before Pilate carried more authority than a thousand defenses.

The Contrast of Two Queens

The literary symmetry of the book becomes strikingly clear once again through the story of two queens, two postures, and two outcomes.

Vashti stands in defiance, asserting her dignity and losing her crown. Esther stands in surrender, yielding her will and gaining one. Both women are courageous, yet their courage flows in opposite direction and only one posture aligns with God's purpose.

Vashti's defiance exposed human pride whereas Esther's humility revealed God's providence.

Together, they form a mirror through which the entire story reflects: one woman rises through assertion and falls, the other bows in surrender and is lifted.

It is a literary and spiritual reflection of God's unchanging principle: *"He brings down the proud and exalts the humble."* *~Luke 1:52*

The Foreshadow of Christlike Humility

Esther's humility also anticipates the greater humility of Christ Himself.

"Who, being in very nature God, did not consider equality with God something to be grasped, but emptied Himself, taking the form of a servant." ~Philippians 2:6–7

Like Christ, Esther does not grasp for status or control. She descends before she is lifted. Her obedience becomes the doorway to redemption for her people, and a reflection of the One who would later redeem all nations through His own surrender.

This is the paradox of grace in which favor flows not from striving, but from stillness, and power is born through humility, not self-exaltation.

And through the story of Esther, we see again that every act of faith, however quiet, becomes a foreshadow of the greater redemption still to come wherein the King of Glory would lower Himself to lift the world.

The King's Choice

"So Esther was taken to King Ahasuerus into his royal house... and the king loved Esther above all the women, and she obtained grace and favor in his sight more than all the virgins." ~Esther 2:16–17

When Ahasuerus returns from his humiliating defeat against Greece, he is not the same man who once ruled from a throne of pride. The conqueror who sought glory through war now sits subdued, his confidence fractured, his empire still glittering but his spirit dimmed. Into that emptiness, Esther enters.

She asks for nothing beyond the counsel of Hegai, the eunuch who knows what pleases the king. In a world defined by excess, Esther's restraint shines like wisdom. Her favor is not earned through flattery or force but through a quiet grace that distinguishes her from all others.

Twice, she will stand before the king:
- In chapter 2, she is received through meekness and beauty.
- In chapter 5, she is received through boldness and intercession.

Both encounters reveal that true favor rests not on out-ward confidence, but on inward alignment through humility and courage, two sides of the same faith.

Providence in Messy Places

However, it is important to note that what unfolds here is not a fairytale. The Persian harem was a system of oppression masked in luxury where women were taken from their homes, paraded for pleasure, and confined as concubines if not chosen. For Esther, this was not an ascent by choice but an assignment by providence.

By Jewish standards, her circumstances were far from ideal, even scandalous. Yet Scripture neither glorifies nor condemns her position. Instead, it highlights her humility, discernment, and the mysterious favor of God moving within corruption.

So, God's hand often moves in places that human morality cannot reconcile. What looks like compromise becomes the canvas of redemption. And what feels like defilement becomes the ground where grace takes root.

Esther's story tells us that holiness is not about pristine conditions but surrendered hearts. God's presence does not retreat from impurity, it transforms it.

So, from the outside, Esther's placement in the harem seems like compromise. And while the empire believes it is consuming her, in reality, God is infiltrating the empire.

"Even in darkness, light dawns for the upright." ~Psalm 112:4

Notice also, how God does not sanctify Persia's system; He over-rules it. The machinery of human corruption keeps grinding, but within its gears, God continues to plants the seeds of deliverance.

Later in the chapter (v.19), another gathering of women is mentioned. Whether it is administrative reshuffling or ritual consolidation, the text reminds us that the empire's system remains broken, but God's purpose remains unshaken.

So, the Persian harem — a place of exploitation — becomes the unlikely soil of covenant preservation, just as the Roman cross — an instrument of execution — became the instrument of salvation.

What appears to tarnish purity becomes the very act that preserves promise. God does not wait for perfection; He invades imperfection with purpose. We can see this through-out Scripture as He meets people in morally complex places:

- The woman at the well (John 4) — redemption born out of scandal.
- Dinner with sinners (Luke 5:30) — holiness seated at a defiled table.
- Touching the leper (Mark 1:40) — purity overtaking corruption.

Esther, like Christ, subverts the systems of her world. She enters the empire's most compromised space and becomes the vessel of God's preservation for His people.

Both reveal that the kingdom of God is not repelled by brokenness, but rather, it transforms it from within. And where the world prizes strength, power, and prestige, the kingdom of God exalts humility, weakness, and surrender.

"God chose the foolish things of the world to shame the wise; God chose the weak things of the world to shame the strong."
~1 Corinthians 1:27

Esther's ascent mirrors the pattern fulfilled in Christ Himself in which redemption is carried through reversal, and humility triumphs over power.

Mordecai's Loyalty

"In those days, while Mordecai sat at the king's gate, two of the king's eunuchs... sought to lay hands on King Ahasuerus." ~Esther 2:21

As Esther settles into her royal role, the narrative returns to Mordecai, still stationed at the gate. His faithful routine becomes the setting for providential setup.

One day, he overhears two eunuchs plotting to assassinate the king. Mordecai reports the plot through Esther, and the culprits are executed. The incident is recorded in the royal chronicles, yet Mordecai receives no reward.

In Persia, such loyalty was normally honored at once. Its omission is no accident. The silence of reward becomes a seed of remembrance. In chapter 6, when the king cannot sleep, he will order this very record to be read. And that moment of "chance" will spark the reversal for Haman's downfall and Mordecai's exaltation.

Even Mordecai's unnoticed faithfulness becomes a tool in God's providence. He does not seek recognition, and so God reserves it for the perfect time.

Faith often feels forgotten before it is remembered.

But the Lord keeps His own record.

Historical Note: The Gallows

When the text later speaks of "gallows," it refers to the Persian practice of impalement — a brutal display meant to deter rebellion. Ancient historian Herodotus confirms this method as a favored form of execution by Persian rulers.

Yet even this grisly image becomes a symbol of spiritual irony. The very weapon built for the righteous becomes the downfall of the wicked. The empire that prides itself on justice will soon display its corruption upon its own gallows.

Such reversals remind us that God's justice is poetic, and that it returns the deeds of the wicked upon their own design.

CLOSING REMARKS

As the story progresses, the reader is invited to look beneath the surface, and to search out the hidden depth beneath the text. Reading between the lines becomes an act of discovery, where mystery waits for those hungry enough to seek it. For the deeper you dig, the more you find that Scripture not only feeds the soul but awakens a new hunger altogether.

This is the paradox of faith itself. Jesus urged His followers to seek the Kingdom of God, a realm spiritual in nature, yet tangible in reality. Those around Him struggled to understand that such a kingdom was not distant but present within, among, and in their midst. Like Nicodemus, who could not grasp the meaning of being born again, they were being invited into a new way of seeing altogether.

In this Kingdom, the old self is put away so that the righteousness of Christ might be put on. The crucifixion of the flesh gives rise to the exaltation of the spirit. Jesus not only revealed this reality; He modeled it, showing us that rebirth is not a metaphor, but a transformation of the whole self, especially our sight.

And this, I believe, is the invitation extended through the book of Esther. Beneath every detail lies a profound contrast — the flesh against the spirit, the pride of man against the heart of God — and through that tension, the nature of Christ is exalted again and again. Pride is cast down so that humility may rise. Holiness shines through corruption. The foolish things of the world shame the wise.

For He is the Beginning and the End, the Lion and the Lamb, the King who lowers Himself as a servant. He takes the weakness of man and turns it into the stage upon which His strength is revealed.

These paradoxes defy human reason, yet they exist because Christ Himself is the fulfillment of them all. In Him, the flesh and the spirit converge; and in Him, the story of Esther finds its song.

And so, we too are invited to read not only the story in the natural, but the one unfolding in the supernatural, and to see the visible world as the veil through which the invisible Kingdom shines.

REFLECTION & DISCUSSION

1. Esther's year of preparation took place out of sight, marked by waiting and submission rather than visible progress.

   How might God be refining you in seasons when it seems like nothing is happening? What does "beauty preparation" look like in the spirit?

2. Esther's restraint distinguished her from others who sought to impress the king.

   When have you been tempted to grasp prematurely for something God promised? What would it look like to trust His timing the way Esther did?

3. God used an unjust system (the Persian harem) to position Esther for redemption.

   How does this challenge your understanding of where and how God can work? Have you ever seen Him bring purpose out of a situation that seemed morally tangled or unfair?

4. Mordecai told Esther to conceal her heritage until the right time.

What part of your calling or identity might God be asking you to keep hidden for a season? How can obedience in silence be as faithful as obedience in action?

5. Mordecai's good deed was recorded but unrewarded until the perfect moment.

   How do you respond when faithfulness goes unnoticed or unrewarded? What might God be writing in the "record book" of your own obedience that will resurface in His timing.

INTERLUDE: THE RETURN OF AMALEK

God's Covenant War from Genesis to Calvary

When we open the book of Esther, it is as though we pull one shimmering thread from an immense tapestry. The more we trace it, the more it winds through other stories across generations, kingdoms, and covenants until the image it reveals is none other than Christ Himself.

What begins in the Persian court does not remain confined there. Esther's story, wrapped in royal intrigue and exile, is part of a far older conflict; one that reaches back to the garden of Eden and stretches forward to the cross. Beneath the political tension between Mordecai and Haman lies a spiritual war as old as humanity itself: the enmity between the seed of the woman and the seed of the serpent (Genesis 3:15).

Two Bloodlines Converge

Esther 3:1 introduces us to Haman, the son of Hammedatha, the Agagite. That single genealogical note carries more weight than it first appears.

It stands in deliberate contrast to a lineage already given:

- Mordecai, descendant of Kish, a Benjamite (Esther 2:5)
- Haman, descendant of Agag, king of the Amalekites (Esther 3:1)

These two names—Kish and Agag—span across the centuries, pulling us back to 1 Samuel 15, where King Saul, son of Kish, was commanded to destroy Amalek completely. Yet Saul disobeyed, sparing King Agag and the best of the spoil. His partial obedience became the seedbed of future devastation.

That unfinished command left an open wound in Israel's story. A war paused, not ended. And the book of Esther reopens it.

Now, in exile, when Mordecai the Benjamite stands against Haman the Agagite, the reader is not witnessing a new feud, but the reawakening of an ancient one. The battle Saul failed to finish resurfaces in Persia.

So, Haman is not a random villain. He is the living remnant of a spiritual hostility that has never slept.

The Amalekite Thread

To grasp the weight of this enmity, we must return to the beginning—Exodus 17—where Amalek first appears in Scripture.

As Israel journeys from Egypt through the wilderness, Amalek ambushes them at Rephidim, striking from behind, preying on the weary and the weak (Deuteronomy 25:17–19). The attack is cowardly, unprovoked, and utterly without mercy.

And in response, God issues a decree that will span generations: *"The Lord will have war with Amalek from generation to generation." (Exodus 17:16)*

This is no tribal quarrel. It is a divine declaration. Amalek becomes the living symbol of rebellion against God's covenant and the relentless enemy of His redemptive plan. Each time Amalek reappears, it carries the same spiritual signature, the same defiance, the same hatred for the chosen line through which the Messiah would come.

The pattern is unmistakable:

- Exodus 17: Amalek attacks Israel's weakest.
- Deuteronomy 25: God commands His people never to forget Amalek's cruelty.
- 1 Samuel 15: Saul fails to destroy Amalek, sparing Agag.
- Esther 3: Haman the Agagite rises, plotting the annihilation of the Jews.

Each appearance is another attempt by darkness to cut off the covenant seed. And so, Haman's rage is not born of wounded pride alone, it is the reincarnation of ancient hatred. Amalek has returned, cloaked in Persian robes, waging the same old war against the purposes of God.

The Spiritual Continuum

Through this lens, the conflict in Esther unfolds on two levels:

- In the natural: an empire's power struggle.
- In the spiritual: a covenant war between light and darkness.

This is the thread the author wants the reader to see. Every act of pride, every decree of destruction, every moment of deliverance is part of that eternal struggle between the serpent and the promise.

The story of Esther, then, is not an isolated account of survival, it is a chapter in the long war for redemption, one that will ultimately find its resolution at the cross.

The Ancient War Beneath the Text

Beneath the political tension of Esther lies an older and deeper conflict, one that predates Persia, predates Saul, and even predates Israel itself. When Scripture unveils the rise of Amalek, it is not introducing a new enemy but revisiting an ancient one.

If we trace the thread backward, we find its roots in the primeval wars of Genesis. In Genesis 14, Abraham wages battle against a coalition of eastern kings who had conquered the region and taken Lot captive. Among the territories subdued in that campaign were the lands of ancient peoples: the Rephaim, the Zuzim, the Emim, the Amorites, and even the Amalekites.

These names echo through the later conquests of Moses, Joshua, and David. Their repetition is intentional. It tells us that Israel's battles were never random acts of territorial expansion; they were confrontations with entrenched spiritual powers.

When God commanded Israel to destroy certain nations, it was not *ethnic cleansing*—it was *spiritual cleansing*. The conquest narratives were not arbitrary violence but judgments upon peoples whose corruption had reached its fullness in which the tribes were steeped in occult worship, blood sacrifice, and rebellion against the Creator.

The land had become polluted by three layers of defilement:

- Idolatry — the worship of fallen powers such as Baal, Ashtoreth, and Molech.
- Occult ritual — ceremonies rooted in blood and demonic invocation.
- Corrupted bloodlines — remnants of hybridized giants, the Nephilim legacy that perpetuated rebellion.

Even centuries later, during David's reign, the Amalekites reappear as symbols of a hatred that cannot die (1 Samuel 30; 2 Samuel 1). The war was never ultimately about geography; it was about authority. Who rules the earth: the rebellious seed or the redemptive seed?

Every stronghold Israel tore down and every city subdued became a physical sign of a deeper reality in which God was reclaiming sacred ground from spiritual occupation. These nations embodied more than human resistance; they represented cosmic opposition to the covenant promise.

The "giants in the land" were more than physical anomalies; they were visible manifestations of invisible corruption—the same spiritual defiance that would one day animate Haman's hatred and, ultimately, incite the crucifixion of Christ Himself.

The Prophetic War of the Seeds

Why does this matter? Because the book of Esther is not an isolated historical episode, it is prophetic in scope. Every moment in her story repeats a promise first spoken in Eden, and a decree that frames the entire narrative of Scripture.

"I will put enmity between you and the woman, and between your seed and her seed; he shall bruise your head, and you shall bruise his heel." ~ Genesis 3:15

This single verse is the seedbed of all redemption. It introduces two spiritual lineages that run through every generation: the seed of the woman, leading to the Messiah, and the seed of the serpent, perpetuating rebellion.

What unfolds in Esther is one chapter in that ongoing war. When Haman the Agagite plots to annihilate the Jews, it is not mere ethnic hostility, it is a satanic attempt to sever the covenant line through which the Redeemer would come.

The tension between Mordecai and Haman, then, is not simply political. It is the continuation of that primordial struggle; the serpent striking at the heel of the seed, and God preparing once again to crush its head through spiritual reversal.

The Seed of the Serpent: The Genesis 6 Pattern

To see the depth of this warfare, Scripture invites us still further back—to *Genesis 6*, where the serpent's strategy takes a darker turn.

"When men began to multiply on the face of the earth, and daughters were born to them, the sons of God saw that the daughters of men were beautiful, and they took wives for themselves, whomever they chose." ~Genesis 6:1–2

From this illicit union came the *Nephilim*; giant offspring whose violence filled the earth. The text says, "All flesh had corrupted its way on the earth," but Noah "was perfect in his generations" (v. 9). That phrase, used elsewhere of unblemished sacrifices, refers not to moral perfection but to wholeness, and to a lineage preserved from the spreading corruption.

Here the pattern begins:

- God preserves a pure line through which the Messiah will come.
- The adversary seeks to corrupt or destroy it through unnatural means.

The rebellion of Genesis 6 was not only moral but cosmic, an attempt by fallen beings to pollute creation itself and sever the covenant line before it could bear fruit. Humanity's defilement became so complete that judgment by flood was both mercy and renewal.

Ancient tradition and early Church commentary recognized this event as the origin of spiritual warfare in human history. The dis-embodied spirits of those violent giants, they said, became the wandering demons of later ages; restless, and opposing God's image wherever it appeared.

And thus, the same corruption that began before the flood resurfaces again through Amalek, through Haman, and through every system that seeks to exalt pride against God's purpose.

What we see, then, in Esther is not merely history, it is prophecy wrapped in narrative. The serpent's war continues, but so does God's promise. Each chapter becomes a rehearsal of redemption, leading ever closer to the moment when the Seed Himself—Christ—will crush the serpent once and for all.

ESTHER AND THE COVENANT WAR

The Unfinished War: From Saul to Esther

The thread of Amalek does not disappear after Exodus, it weaves its way through the entire Old Testament like a dark vein of resistance.

God's declaration in Exodus 17:16— *"The Lord will have war with Amalek from generation to generation"*—is not hyperbole; it is prophecy. It is the reminder of Eden's first decree of enmity, now carried into history.

One generation after another takes up the conflict:

- Joshua fought Amalek at Rephidim while Moses lifted weary hands toward heaven.
- Saul, son of Kish, was commanded to destroy Amalek completely (1 Samuel 15), but disobeyed—sparing King Agag.
- Samuel, the prophet, called that disobedience rebellion and com-pared it to witchcraft, then finished what Saul would not.
- Yet remnants survived, and centuries later, Haman the Agagite arises in Persia—the living embodiment of that unfinished war.

Thus, the book of Esther is not a new conflict but a continuation. It is the same enmity that began in Eden, resurfacing through the ages in the form of: covenant vs corruption, faith vs pride, light vs darkness.

What Saul left incomplete, God resolves through exile and providence, and through a woman who will stand where kings once fell short.

Echoes in the Ministry of Jesus

But the war does not end in the Old Testament, it simply changes form. By the time Jesus walks the earth, the giants are gone, but the spirits behind them remain. The serpent's seed no longer wields spears or swords; it hides in the shadows: in fear, infirmity, and oppression.

Christ meets them head-on.

Many of His most dramatic confrontations take place in the Decapolis and Bashan—regions once ruled by giants.

- In the tombs of the Gerasene demoniac (*Mark 5:1–20*), a man possessed by a legion of spirits shrieks in the darkness.

- Around Capernaum and Caesarea Philippi, centers of pagan worship built atop ancient strongholds, He silences unclean powers.

Bashan was infamous in the Old Testament as the haunt of the Rephaim—descendants of those ancient tyrants. It is no coincidence that Jesus performed more exorcisms there than anywhere else. He was reclaiming the very ground that had once symbolized demonic rule.

When He stood at Caesarea Philippi and declared, *"On this rock I will build My church, and the gates of Hades shall not prevail against it," (Matthew 16:18)*

He spoke those words in the shadow of Mount Hermon—the mountain Jewish tradition associated with the descent of the fallen sons of God. There, on the very soil where rebellion was said to have begun, Christ announced its end. So, it was not metaphor. It was conquest.

The Greater Joshua and the Greater David

From Joshua to David, Israel fought visible enemies through giants, strongholds, and nations fortified against the promise. Each victory was only a shadow of the greater one to come.

- Joshua (*Yehoshua*) conquered the land.
- David conquered the giants.
- Jesus (*Yeshua*) conquered death itself.

He is the true and greater warrior who enters the strong man's house and binds him (*Matthew 12:29*).

The physical sword of Joshua cleansed the land; the sword of the Spirit (*Ephesians 6:17*) now cleanses hearts and atmospheres.

So, the gospel does more than rescue souls, it dethrones rulers. Every salvation is an act of warfare; every conversion, a declaration that another territory has changed hands.

The Descent and the Proclamation

But the victory of Christ did not end at the cross, it descended beneath it. Peter writes that Jesus *"went and made proclamation to the spirits in prison"* (*1 Peter 3:19–22*)—a statement of triumph spoken into the depths where those ancient rebels were bound.

He descended as conqueror, not captive, proclaiming that the war was over. Then He ascended, enthroned above every principality and power, visible and invisible. Thus, the covenant war reaches its ultimate resolution:

- What began in Eden is fulfilled at Golgotha.
- The serpent that deceived Eve is crushed beneath the heel of her promised Seed.

- The strongholds of Bashan fall before the risen Christ.

So, the war that stretched from Genesis to Persia, from Amalek to Haman, finds its climax in the empty tomb.

The Ongoing War and Our Victory

And yet the conflict continues, not in blood and soil, but in spirit.

"For we wrestle not against flesh and blood, but against principalities, powers, the rulers of darkness, and spiritual hosts of wickedness in the heavenly places." ~ Ephesians 6:12

The book of Esther is therefore not confined to history; rather, it is a living mirror of our own age. The same war of seeds plays out still, only now the battlefield is the human heart.

Every act of obedience, every hidden prayer, every word of intercession participates in this same supernatural campaign. Like Esther, believers today are positioned by providence in a world of supernatural warfare. And like her, our calling is not mere survival but intercession; to stand in Christ's authority and extend His victory into the present age.

Her story becomes our also in which the God who preserved His people through one woman's humility now empowers His Church through His Spirit. The battle belongs to the Lord still, but the scepter of authority has been placed in our hands.

CLOSING REMARKS

As we read through Scripture, it's easy to compartmentalize stories like Esther into isolated moments in time. Logically, we know they are all interconnected, but practically, unless we go out of our way to piece everything together, we tend to get lost in the minutiae of hard-to-pronounce locations and long lists of genealogies that are even harder to pronounce.

And more often than not, we'd rather skim over all those names and places that we'll probably forget in the next five minutes anyway, just to get to the parts that really speak to us in terms of spiritual application and growth.

I say this because when I say *we*, I really mean *me*. That's been my approach for most of my life. Only in recent years have I learned to take a different approach altogether.

But the truth is, the book of Esther is a prime example of how much we can miss when we're not paying attention. Even a single name, mentioned only in passing, can send us spiraling down a path we never realized was there—one that opens a depth and magnitude of Scripture, and of God's character, we never thought possible.

The deeper you go, the more of God's mystery begins to unfold, until you realize just how alive His Word truly is. You find that you're not merely studying one isolated account of His sovereignty, but gazing into a microcosm of time, and a story that spans the breadth of Scripture as it reveals its living implications for the reality in which we now walk as the body of Christ.

I am constantly amazed and in awe of how deeply masterful God's authorship truly is, and how the story of redemption is written with such intricate design. The characters and contexts may vary from one book to the next, but the narrative remains the same. And those words spoken, *"I knew you before the foundations of the earth,"* take on a meaning far more beautiful and profound than we could have realized.

The way people and places intersect across time—from Genesis all the way to the Cross—could only be orchestrated and authored by the One who is the Word Himself. Suddenly, every name or location mentioned becomes like a breadcrumb, leading you down a trail of grand design toward a story much richer than you ever anticipated.

Each person, however obscure they may seem, plays a pivotal role. Each location marks a conquest of far greater magnitude. And by the time Jesus steps into His ministry, no stone has been left unturned.

Everything meets its culmination and fulfillment in Jesus Christ. The words that marked the beginning of a war in Genesis carry themselves as the foundation for everything that unfolds throughout the Old Testament and beyond.

Esther likely had no idea how she fit into the magnitude of such a story. While her role as the physical means of deliverance for her people cannot be overstated, the pivotal role she played in the cosmic battle behind the scenes is, in my opinion, even more magnificent. Because she was not only the physical means of deliverance, but also the supernatural instrument through which God preserved the line of the Deliverer Himself. And through Him, the salvation of the entire world.

The enemy she faced in her day is the very same one we face now—only today, Christ has already claimed the victory. For Esther, the battle in her lifetime was for survival. For us, the battle now is for glory.

REFLECTION & DISCUSSION

1. What does it mean for you personally that the war between the seed of the woman and the seed of the serpent still rages today, yet from a place of Christ's finished victory?

   How can you live from victory rather than striving for it?

2. What are the modern "strongholds of Bashan" in your life or culture (places long claimed by darkness) that God is asking you to reclaim through prayer and declaration?

3. Esther's story reveals that unseen battles are won in hidden places.

   How can you cultivate a lifestyle of hidden warfare, where prayer, fasting, and obedience move unseen kingdoms?

4. Saul's failure to obey fully opened a door that Esther later had to close.

   What areas of incomplete obedience in your life might be leaving footholds for the enemy's influence?

5. When Jesus said, "The gates of Hades will not prevail," He was declaring offense, not defense.

    What does it look like for you to move from surviving attacks to advancing territory in your spiritual walk?

CHAPTER THREE

Haman's Rise

*After these things King Ahasuerus praised Haman the son of
Hammedatha the Agagite, and promoted him, and set his seat above
all the officials who were with him. ~Esther 3:1*

The third chapter opens with what seems to be a routine act
of political advancement, yet beneath this scene of royal favor lies
one of the most significant theological pivots in the book.

We've already traced, in the previous interlude, the ancient
thread connecting Mordecai and Haman back to the unfinished
war between Saul and Agag—the confrontation between covenant
promise and perpetual rebellion. That groundwork now becomes
vital, for the text deliberately reawakens that same hostility here
through one subtle phrase: *"Haman the Agagite."*

The author expects the reader to remember what this means.
This is not merely a surname, but a signal, and a reminder that the
spirit of Amalek has resurfaced once again in the Persian court.
The conflict that began in Exodus and bled through the days of
Saul now finds new form in Susa's palace. The war that once raged
with swords now manifests through spirit, blood, and allegiance.

The writer also places this moment *after* the elevation of Esther, almost as if to show that God's redemptive plan and the enemy's retaliation always move in parallel. Each advance of God's purpose awakens opposition, and each rising of light summons its shadow.

In Haman, Amalek is reborn through ancient hatred dressed in royal authority. In Mordecai, covenant faithfulness stands quietly at the gate, unmoved, and unwavering. What Saul once failed to complete through disobedience, God will now finish through obedience born in exile.

The scene, then, is far more than political reshuffling. It is the rekindling of a cosmic war via the ancient enmity between the seed of the serpent and the seed of promise, now playing out on the stage of Persia.

The difference is that this time, the victory will not come through conquest, but through courage. And not through the might of armies, but through the faithfulness of two exiles whose quiet obedience will shift the course of kingdoms.

Mordecai and Esther: Concealment and Revelation

"All the king's servants, when they were at the king's gate, bowed or paid homage to Haman since the king had commanded it. Mordecai, however, never bowed or paid homage... for Mordecai had told them that he was a Jew." ~Esther 3:2-4

As the story unfolds, the two central figures of faith—Mordecai and Esther—emerge as reflections of God's own hidden and revealed nature. Both walk in obedience, yet their obedience takes opposing forms.

Mordecai stands in the open court, publicly identified as a Jew. He refuses to bow before Haman, even under the weight of imperial expectation. His defiance is not arrogance; it is allegiance. His posture of resistance becomes the visible expression of covenant loyalty in a land that has long forgotten God.

Esther, however, moves in the opposite rhythm. By Mordecai's counsel, she conceals her Jewish identity. She navigates the Persian court with quiet discernment and her faith hidden beneath the garments of assimilation. Her obedience is no less real, only less visible.

This duality is deliberate. The author wants the reader to see that God's redemptive plan requires both kinds of obedience:

- The boldness that stands in the open gate.
- The wisdom that waits behind closed doors.

Mordecai's faith is a light that refuses to dim before men, whereas Esther's is a flame kept hidden until the appointed hour. One bears witness through resistance; the other, through restraint. And yet both are aligned beneath the same spiritual hand where one is seen, the other concealed.

Together, they reflect the mystery of God Himself: A God who sometimes speaks through thunder and sometimes hides in silence, yet never ceases to move.

Mordecai's Counsel and Esther's Timing

When Mordecai instructed Esther not to reveal her heritage (2:10), it was not cowardice, it was wisdom born of discernment.

The Persian court was volatile, unpredictable, and easily swayed by envy and intrigue. To reveal her identity too soon would have endangered not only Esther's life but also the redemptive position God was building for her.

In this, Mordecai's counsel mirrors God's own pattern of concealment throughout the book. Just as the Lord's name remains unspoken, His plan remains hidden until the moment of revelation. So too, Esther's silence becomes prophetic as it mirrors the silence of God Himself, who withholds His un-veiling until the appointed time.

Concealment, therefore, is not compromise, it is strategy. God often hides His deliverers within the very systems meant to destroy them.

In due season, what is hidden will be revealed. The same Esther who now remains silent will one day stand before the king and speak the truth that changes everything. Her concealment therefore is not the absence of calling; it is its incubation. Until then, she waits. And in her waiting, God is further revealed.

Mordecai's Public Declaration of Identity

When the royal command required all to bow before Haman, Mordecai refused. The text gives us the reason: *"For he had told them that he was a Jew." (Esther 3:4)*

Those few words shift everything. Mordecai's defiance is no longer a matter of personal pride or civil disobedience; it becomes an act of spiritual allegiance. His refusal is not rebellion against authority but reverence toward covenant. To bow before Haman, a descendant of Agag, would be to symbolically bow before Amalek, the ancient enemy of God's people and of God Himself.

In that moment, Mordecai's loyalty is tested not in warfare but in worship. Like Daniel before the golden image or the apostles before the Sanhedrin, Mordecai stands where obedience to man collides with obedience to God.

"We must obey God rather than men." ~Acts 5:29

Here at the gate, the war of the ages surfaces once again. A single man's refusal draws into the open what has been warring beneath history's surface since Eden. So, his "no" becomes more than resistance, it becomes remembrance. In that act of stillness, Mordecai reaffirms that covenant allegiance will not bow to counterfeit authority.

Hidden and Revealed: The Pattern of Divine Strategy

By now, the reader begins to recognize a pattern woven throughout the story, and an interplay between concealment and revelation, silence and speech, hiddenness and boldness.

Esther and Mordecai move in opposite rhythms, yet both are precisely aligned to God's design. Esther conceals her identity; Mordecai declares his. She hides for the sake of timing; he stands for the sake of truth. Both are faithful, and both are necessary.

Esther's concealment secures her access to power. Mordecai's defiance exposes the adversary. Together, they form a single strategy of spiritual intelligence; one advancing quietly from with-in, the other standing firmly from without.

The same pattern is mirrored in the character of God through-out the book:

- His *name* is hidden, yet His *sovereignty* is unmistakable.
- His *voice* is silent, yet His *hand* moves through every scene.

Faith, then, takes many faces but only one form: surrender. Whether through Esther's quiet restraint or Mordecai's open bold-ness, both reveal that obedience is not measured by visibility but by alignment. What matters is not how faith looks, but Whose will it serves.

When the moment of revelation finally comes, the hidden and the revealed converge through her silence and his stand meeting in perfect harmony. That is how deliverance is born: when obedience in secret meets obedience in sight.

This is also the pattern of spiritual warfare in what is hidden is being prepared, and what is revealed is being tested, when both submit to God's timing as redemption manifests in full view.

The Fury of Haman

"And when Haman saw that Mordecai bowed not, nor did him reverence, then was Haman full of wrath. But he thought scorn to lay hands on Mordecai alone... therefore Haman sought to destroy all the Jews that were throughout the whole kingdom." ~Esther 3:5–6

The text then escalates quickly from offense to obsession. Haman's fury is far greater than the provocation warrants. His reaction is not merely emotional, it is spiritual. Behind his rage burns the same hatred that has stalked the covenant line since

Genesis 3:15, where enmity was decreed between the seed of the woman and the seed of the serpent.

What enrages Haman is not Mordecai's insolence but his *identity.* The very presence of a faithful Jew exposes the darkness that hides behind power. This is why the text records that Haman "thought scorn to lay hands on Mordecai alone." His fury metastasizes into genocide because spiritual hatred never stays small, it always seeks total annihilation.

So, Mordecai's refusal becomes a prophetic act of rest-oration. Where Saul once spared Agag and forfeited his crown, Mordecai stands firm and completes the battle, not through sword or bloodshed, but through faith and endurance. The unfinished war is being settled not on the field, but at the gate.

In other words, Mordecai's stillness fulfills what Saul's sword could not.

The Casting of Lots: Providence Over Paganism

"In the first month, that is, the month Nisan, in the twelfth year of King Ahasuerus, they cast Pur, that is, the lot, before Haman from day to day and from month to month, until the twelfth month, that is, the month Adar." ~Esther 3:7

With vengeance conceived in his heart, Haman turns to the occult traditions of Persia to seal his plan. He seeks the favor of false gods through divination and the casting of *Pur*, the lot. The phrase *"from day to day and from month to month"* suggests a drawn-out ritual, a repetition of omens and superstitions, as priests and astrologers sought the "right" alignment for destruction.

In other words, Haman is not merely choosing a date, he is attempting to manipulate destiny. The longer he casts, the more desperate his striving becomes. Paganism always exhausts itself trying to control what only providence commands.

Yet even here, God reigns, and the lot falls not by chance, but by decree.

So, the same God who remains silent in the story governs the very dice that Haman throws. And what Haman believes to be superstition becomes submission to God's sovereignty.

The month chosen—Adar—will ultimately mark not Israel's destruction, but their deliverance. And the decree born of hatred will now become the day of reversal. So, even in the practices of witchcraft and wrath, God still rules the calendar.

The Practice of Casting Lots

In the Achaemenid empire, *Pur* (plural *Purim*) referred to small inscribed stones, carved bones, or clay fragments used in divination — ancient "dice" believed to reveal the will of the gods. The process was sacred to the Persians, a ritual of superstition cloaked in ceremony.

Haman's method likely followed a two-step system common to the royal astrologers of the time:

1. Casting for the month — twelve marked lots, one for each month of the year, were drawn. → The lot fell on Adar, the twelfth month.

2. Casting for the day — lots representing individual days were then drawn. → It landed on the thirteenth day of Adar (cf. Esther 3:13; 9:1).

Persian diviners would repeat the ritual multiple times to confirm the omen. Once a consistent result appeared, they believed the gods had spoken. But in heaven's court, the decree was already sealed long before Haman's hand reached the urn.

So, what seemed to him like chance was in fact choreography, and the ultimate sovereignty of God was directing even the dice of the enemy.

The Irony of Sovereignty

To the Persians, the casting of lots was sacred divination. Yet, to the God of Israel, it was strategy. Haman thought he was consulting fate, but fate itself bowed to the God of Israel. Every throw of his hand advanced a story already written by God. So, heaven was not reacting to Haman's schemes, it was repurposing them in which the hands of rebellion were still the instruments of redemption.

Mercy Disguised as Coincidence

The lot fell on the twelfth month — *Adar* — nearly a full year away. To Haman, this delay was convenient, a generous window to organize destruction across the empire. But in God's economy, the delay was mercy.

That span of eleven months became the buffer where redemption would ripen. Within that time, God would orchestrate:

- Esther's courage to mature (Chapters 4–5)

- Mordecai's remembrance and exaltation (Chapter 6)
- Israel's deliverance through reversal (Chapters 8–9)

Had the lot fallen sooner, there would have been no time for salvation to unfold.

So the "random delay" was God's restraint. Even in a pagan ritual, heaven carved out a window of grace. Therefore, the casting of lots became an altar of sovereignty and a place where demonic timing was overruled by covenant mercy.

Why the Twelfth Month of Adar?

In Hebrew symbolism, *Adar* carries prophetic weight. It is the twelfth and final month of the biblical calendar, and a number representing completion, transition, and reversal. As the year closes with *Adar*, so does the narrative of Esther, yet not in death, but in deliverance. And what the enemy declared as an end became God's declaration of beginning.

The very month chosen for destruction would later become a memorial of joy through the Feast of *Purim*, named after the lots the enemy cast. So, the instruments of annihilation became the emblems of celebration, and the day appointed for mourning became the day of gladness.

"You meant evil against me, but God meant it for good."
~Genesis 50:20

This is the great irony of redemption in which the enemy rolls for ruin, and God writes redemption.

The Spiritual Undercurrent

Haman's ritual of divination was intended to align him with false gods, but it only furthered the purposes of the true One. This is the unchanging irony of rebellion in which every demonic attempt to control destiny becomes the very instrument through which God displays His sovereignty. Through this act we glimpse the mystery of providence in motion:

- Haman casts lots in pride.
- God uses them to mark the countdown to deliverance.
- Every turn of the dice moves history closer to redemption.

As one rabbi later wrote, *"The dice were in Haman's hands, but the table belonged to God."* And so, it remains that no decree of hell, no manipulation of time, and no counsel of darkness can outrun the wisdom of the Lord. So, what the enemy rolls in arrogance, God redirects in grace.

Providence Over Probability

The narrator also draws deliberate attention to Haman's obsessive repetition: *"From day to day, and from month to month..."* ~Esther 3:7

This rhythmic phrase paints Haman as restless and superstitious, a man enslaved to the illusion of control. Each ritual, each casting, and each consultation with his gods only exposes the futility of human striving to manufacture destiny apart from the Creator.

The irony is that Haman believes he is discerning fate, while every movement of his hand fulfills God's own design.

The Biblical Pattern of Casting Lots

It's also important to note that casting lots was not unique to Persia, as it appears throughout Scripture as a sacred symbol of divine decision.

Yet the difference is striking:

- In pagan culture, lots were cast to *control* fate.
- In covenant faith, lots were cast to *submit* to God's will.
- So, where the world manipulates, the people of God yield.
- Throughout Scripture, the lot becomes an act of trust, not chance:
- Dividing the Promised Land — *Joshua 18:6–10*
- Choosing the scapegoat on the Day of Atonement — *Leviticus 16:8–10*
- Revealing Achan's hidden sin — *Joshua 7:14*
- Assigning priestly duties in the Temple — *1 Chronicles 24:5–19*
- Identifying Jonah's guilt at sea — *Jonah 1:7*

In each case, the lot was not a gamble, but a confession and an acknowledgment that the outcome belongs to God alone. It was not used to *decide* His will, but to *surrender* to it.

So, where the pagan casts to command an outcome, the believer casts to release it. This is the difference between fate and faith.

From the Lot to the Spirit

This same principle of spiritual guidance through the surrender of human control to the will of God appears one final time in Scripture.

Before the outpouring of the Holy Spirit at Pentecost, the apostles gathered to fill the vacancy left by Judas. In prayer and unity, they sought the Lord's choice between two men, Matthias and Joseph Barsabbas.

"And they prayed and said, 'You, Lord, who know the hearts of all, show which one of these two You have chosen.' Then they cast lots for them, and the lot fell on Matthias." ~Acts 1:24–26

Notice the sequence: they prayed first, then cast lots. Even here, the act was not superstition, but submission.

Yet this moment also marks a spiritual threshold in which it is the final time lots appear in Scripture. Immediately after, in Acts 2, the Holy Spirit descends, and from that moment onward, the people of God are no longer led by physical tokens, but by the indwelling Spirit Himself.

Where once they cast lots to discern the will of God, they would now walk in daily communion with the God who now dwells within them. So, the age of casting had passed, and the age of indwelling had begun.

Guidance After Pentecost

After the coming of the Spirit, God's direction took on a new and intimate form. God no longer spoke through stones or dice but through hearts filled with His presence.

Scripture reveals this new order of guidance:

- The voice of the Spirit — *"Set apart for Me Barnabas and Saul." (Acts 13:2)*

- Prophecy and spiritual gifts — The Spirit distributing wisdom, knowledge, and discernment (*1 Corinthians 12–14*).
- The unity of the Body — *"It seemed good to the Holy Spirit and to us..." (Acts 15:28)*

What was once external guidance has become internal communion. The same God who governed the fall of Haman's lots now governs the beating of a Spirit-filled heart. So, where Haman sought direction from fate, the believer now receives direction from the Spirit. And where the enemy rolled dice to destroy, the saints are led by the voice of the Shepherd to deliver.

"In all your ways acknowledge Him, and He will direct your paths." ~Proverbs 3:6

The Literary Irony

The author of Esther places Haman's ritual of divination at the center of this chapter not to dignify it, but to expose it. In this way, Esther 3 becomes a miniature gospel. The enemy plots destruction, but heaven weaves deliverance into the very threads of his decree.

"The lot is cast into the lap, but its every decision is from the Lord." ~Proverbs 16:33

The Eve of Passover

Even the date of Haman's decree bears prophetic weight. Esther 3:12 records that the royal scribes were summoned on the *thirteenth day of Nisan* which was the eve of Passover.

The very next night, Jews across the empire would be preparing to remember their deliverance from Egypt—the night the blood of the lamb shielded their households as the angel of death passed over. (*Exodus 12*)

And yet, on that same eve, another empire was sealing a decree of death against those same covenant people.

Note the irony:

- On the night meant to celebrate *freedom from death*, a new *sentence of death* was written.
- While Israel prepared to purge leaven from their homes, Persia filled its palace with corruption.
- As God once judged Egypt's pride, He now prepared to overturn Persia's.

So, what Pharaoh began with chains, Haman attempted with ink. Yet both met the same end.

The decree of death was written on the night of deliverance, ensuring that Passover would replay itself in exile. And centuries later, that same pattern would reach its climax at the Cross when, on another Passover eve, the true Lamb of God was condemned to die, that all nations might live.

Where Haman's decree sought the death of a nation, the Father's decree through Christ secured the salvation of *all* nations.

In both stories, timing was not coincidence; it was prophecy. Even beneath the ink of a pagan edict, the rhythm of redemption continued to beat. In other words, the same God who passed over His people in Egypt was still passing over them in Persia.

The Price of Genocide

"If it please the king, let it be decreed that they be destroyed; and I will pay ten thousand talents of silver into the hands of those who carry out the king's business..." ~Esther 3:9

Haman's proposal is as chilling as it is calculated. He offers to pay *ten thousand talents of silver*—a sum equal to nearly two-thirds of the Persian Empire's annual revenue.

Historian Herodotus estimates the empire's income at fifteen to twenty thousand talents per year. One talent weighed roughly seventy-five pounds, meaning Haman's bribe equaled more than 340 metric tons of silver, billions in modern value.

This was not a gift. It was a purchase, and transaction to buy the right to commit genocide.

The empire of Persia, for all its grandeur, sold its soul for silver.

And through that exchange, the author draws our attention to a recurring biblical motif through the *currency of betrayal.*

Silver paid for the lives of the innocent in Esther's day, just as silver later clinked in Judas's hand when he betrayed the Innocent One. The weight of metal mirrors the weight of sin. Both are spent for blood.

But even this, too, is irony. For in the economy of heaven, what man purchases for death, God redeems for life. The price of blood becomes the down payment of grace. And just as the silver of betrayal financed a cross that became our redemption, so the silver of Haman financed a decree that God would overturn into deliverance.

The Source of the Silver

Haman almost certainly did not possess such staggering wealth himself. His promise to pay ten thousand talents of silver was not an act of generosity, it was a projection of profit. The expectation was that the money would come from the plunder of the Jews once they were destroyed.

This practice was common across ancient empires in which the possessions of the condemned reverted to the crown or to the accuser who engineered their downfall. Both decrees in *Esther* confirm this intent: *"To destroy, to kill, and to annihilate all Jews... and to plunder their goods." ~Esther 3:13; cf. 8:11*

Thus, the "ten thousand talents" was not an up-front payment, but a promise financed by blood. It was greed disguised as governance, and a business plan built on genocide. Haman's ambition cloaked evil in the language of economy. His proposal was not only political; it was spiritual manipulation masked as fiscal logic.

Why the Amount Matters

1. Flattery of the King

   Xerxes was known for extravagance and for costly military campaigns that drained his treasury. Haman's offer must have sounded like a solution and an effortless way to refill an empty empire. The bribe appealed to the king's vanity and to his fatigue, flattering both his greed and his pride.

2.   Economic Motive Disguising Evil

The offer made genocide sound rational. Evil wrapped itself in administrative efficiency: *Why not profit from removing a trouble-some people?* It is the same deception that still legitimizes oppression today through profit masquerading as policy, and greed rebranded as order.

3.   Providential Irony

But by the end of the story, the balance sheet reverses: *"That day King Ahasuerus gave the house of Haman, the enemy of the Jews, to Queen Esther."* ~Esther 8:1–2

The very estate and wealth Haman offered as payment are transferred to Esther and Mordecai. What was meant to destroy becomes inheritance, and the price of death becomes the provision of life.

God turns plunder into provision, and the treasury of evil into the funding of redemption.

The Spiritual Undercurrent

Beneath the economics lies a darker exchange. Haman's silver represents the *currency of corruption* and an attempt to purchase legitimacy for evil. It is greed baptized in blood, and power sanctified by profit.

Yet in heaven's economy, such wealth is worthless. What looks persuasive in the court of kings is bankrupt before the throne of God. Haman's offer is immense and impressive, yet it is the clearest example of spiritual poverty disguised as success. His ledger gleams with silver, but his soul is in deficit. So in truth, what appears to be fiscal control is simply the purchase of his own destruction.

False Order Leading to Chaos

The author then closes the chapter with a deliberate symmetry:

- 3:1–2 — Haman is promoted, and the empire commands all to bow.
- 3:15 — The decree is sealed, and the king and Haman sit to drink while the city falls into confusion.

Here, it becomes evident that promotion gives birth to confusion, and false order collapses into chaos. So, what begins as forced reverence ends in disorder. The empire drinks to its own deception, celebrating a peace that does not exist. The streets of Susa tremble beneath the weight of spiritual dissonance as outward stability masks inward collapse.

This is the anatomy of pride: control masking decay, and dominance masquerading as stability. Pride always seeks to create order through power, but its end is confusion. And as Babel fell under its own ambition, so Persia staggers beneath its own pride.

A Counterfeit Covenant

Haman's transaction with the king is also more than just a political bribe, it is a spiritual covenant. By offering silver for blood, he binds greed and hatred together and seals them with royal authority. It is a satanic parody of God's order and a counterfeit covenant where corruption purchases dominion. Yet unseen by all, God had already issued a higher decree.

"The wealth of the sinner is stored up for the righteous."
~Proverbs 13:22

The contract of death was already voided by a covenant of life. And Haman's offer could never buy what God had already claimed. No price can purchase what God has purposed to preserve.

The Shadow of Another Silver

This moment casts a prophetic shadow forward to another dark exchange that took place the night Judas sold the Son of Man for thirty pieces of silver.

They were different empires, but the same spirit. And different amounts, yet the same motive. Both transactions reek of betrayal wrapped in profit.

- Haman purchased death for a nation.
- Judas purchased death for the Savior.
- Both were driven by greed.
- Yet both were overturned by resurrection power.

At Golgotha, the price of genocide meets its antithesis: the sacrifice of One for all.

Where Haman's silver financed destruction, Christ's blood purchased redemption. Where Persia's decree condemned, the decree of heaven justified.

"You were not redeemed with corruptible things, such as silver or gold, but with the precious blood of Christ." ~1 Peter 1:18–19

This is the spiritual inversion at the center of all history in which the economy of man demands payment. Whereas the economy of God gives pardon.

Every coin of Haman's imagined treasury rings hollow against the weight of Calvary's mercy. The lots of destruction become the feast of *Purim*—a celebration of reversal—just as the thirty pieces of betrayal are swallowed up by the priceless blood of the Lamb.

And so, the chapter closes not with despair, but with fore-shadowed victory. The empire drinks in ignorance while the city trembles in confusion. But God has already spoken: Deliverance is on its way.

CLOSING REMARKS

The contrast between Esther's hidden obedience and Mordecai's bold stand of defiance can sometimes lead to the assumption that one expression of faithfulness stands superior to the other. Or that Esther's budding strength is somehow lesser than Mordecai's fortified courage.

It's easy to look at the faithfulness of others and compare ourselves in ways that diminish the very work God is already doing within us. This is the pitfall that so often becomes a stumbling block in our walk, and a weight we were never meant to carry.

The truth is, we place such heavy expectations upon ourselves that we end up writing the script of our own failure before we've even taken the first step. If I think I should be further along than that person over there, there will always be someone else waiting to remind me of how far I've fallen short.

Yet when I look at Christ, He says something altogether different. Where I see failure, He calls me righteous. Where I see shame, He sees me clothed in His perfection. How can this be? How do I reconcile such a contradiction?

Suddenly, I'm faced with a choice to either believe the reflection of my weakness or the revelation of His Word. Because if what I say is true, then Christ is made a liar. But if His words are true, then nothing spoken by my flesh can ever overturn what He has already spoken over me.

Too often we look to the world—or even to our own opinions—to define our standing, when the only verdict that matters, especially above our own, is Christ's. It was His blood that purchased my identity and His cross that secured my righteousness. That means I no longer belong to the flesh, but am clothed in the full righteousness of the One who was slain for me.

And what a cost that was. For if such a price was paid for my redemption, then how could I continue living as though I still belong to the ruin He rescued me from? I have no righteousness of my own to claim and no merit to boast of. Yet in Him, I possess the fullness of what I could never earn.

Where Christ now stands in victory, I also stand, because what He has claimed for Himself, He has also claimed for me.

So, I no longer need to measure my faith against another's. I no longer need to perform holiness to prove belonging. For as long as my eyes remain fixed on the face of my Savior, there is no comparison left to make, only communion with the One who calls me His own.

REFLECTION & DISCUSSION

1. There are seasons when obedience must stay veiled so that it matures in secret, and others when it must stand exposed to confront darkness.

   Where might your obedience right now be *hidden for timing*, like Esther's, and where might it be *called into the light* like Mordecai's, to testify openly before others?

2. Mordecai's "I will not bow" was less about posture and more about allegiance. The bows we offer today often come dressed as prudence, relevance, or strategy.

   What subtle "bows"—to comfort, influence, acceptance, or control—tempt you to trade covenant loyalty for cultural belonging?

3. Haman's silver bought him legitimacy for evil, but our modern coins of currency often look like platform, applause, or performance. Each can sanctify self-promotion under the banner of ministry.

   Where might your pursuit of *measurable success* be masquerading as faithfulness? How can you discern when the fruit you're producing is *kingdom growth* and not *Haman's arithmetic* through multiplication without consecration?

4. The lot was fate in paganism but surrender in Scripture.

    In practice, do you approach decision-making to manage outcomes or to yield outcomes? What would it look like this week to move from control to consecration?

5. Pride creates an appearance of order that ends in confusion (3:15).

    Where might your desire to control people or outcomes be generating hidden chaos, and what would humility require you to release?

CHAPTER FOUR

The Cry at the Gate

When Mordecai learned all that had been done, he tore his clothes and put on sackcloth and ashes, and went out into the midst of the city, crying out with a loud and bitter cry.
~Esther 4:1

The fourth chapter of Esther marks a dramatic shift from hidden preparation to public intercession. The mask of calm order in the Persian Empire is now shattered by the sound of lament, and the unseen war now breaks out into the open.

Mordecai's Response: The Cry of Covenant Grief

When Mordecai hears the decree, notice how he doesn't retreat into silence or plot revenge. Instead, he mourns. He rends his garments, puts on sackcloth and ashes, and raises his voice in the city square. In Jewish custom, this act was the highest form of repentance and grief: a physical embodiment of inner anguish before God.

But this is not mere sorrow. It's prophetic lament. Mordecai is interceding for his people through grief.

In Scripture, sackcloth and ashes always accompany deep spiritual awareness that something in the natural realm has broken alignment with heaven's justice. His cry then isn't political protest, it's spiritual warfare expressed through lamentation.

The Significance of the Gate

The palace gate has been Mordecai's defining boundary through-out the story:

- In Chapter 2, he lingered at the gate to watch over Esther.
- In Chapter 2:21, he overheard the eunuchs' plot to kill the king, a moment of hidden intercession.
- Now in Chapter 4, he stands there again, barred from entry because of his sackcloth.

This gate is both geographical and spiritual, and it stands as a threshold between influence and limitation, visibility and separation.

In earlier chapters, the gate was his post of faithful waiting. Now it becomes his place of intercessory weeping. Mordecai cannot pass through because Persian law forbids mourning garments in the king's presence. Yet that very exclusion reveals something important:

The kingdom of man cannot tolerate visible grief, but the kingdom of God is born through it. And the place that once represented access now becomes a barrier, foreshadowing the tension between the natural and spiritual realms. However, Mordecai is positioned exactly where heaven wants him: at the threshold between despair and breakthrough.

A City in Lament

"And in every province, wherever the king's command and decree reached, there was great mourning among the Jews, with fasting, weeping, and lamenting, and many lay in sackcloth and ashes." ~Esther 4:3

The lament spreads like wildfire. Across the empire, an invisible unity begins to form among God's scattered people. Though exiled, unarmed, and politically powerless, their response is spiritual alignment through fasting and mourning.

Without any prophet, altar, or temple, the Jews return instinctively to the only posture that invites God's intervention through humble desperation. So the people who had no access to the temple now become living altars through lamentation and intercession.

Esther's Isolation: A Palace of Silence

"But Esther's maids and eunuchs came and told her, and the queen was deeply distressed." ~Esther 4:4

The contrast here is haunting. Mordecai is in public lament while Esther is in insulated peace. The queen of Persia—who shares the same blood as the condemned—is the last to know.

The palace, a symbol of luxury and influence, has also become a soundproof prison. This reveals a spiritual principle to us as the reader in which comfort can become a barrier to discernment.

Influence without awareness is impotence disguised as prestige.

Esther's ignorance is not negligence, it's separation. The system she has been elevated into has effectively blinded her to the suffering outside its walls. And it's not until Mordecai's cry pierces that insulation that it reawakens her identity as a covenant daughter rather than a Persian queen.

The Theology of Lament: Hidden Power in Mourning

Throughout Scripture, lament is not weakness, it is invitation.

- When Nineveh mourned, judgment was delayed.
- When Hannah wept, a prophet was conceived.
- When Mordecai wailed, a deliverer was awakened.

Mourning, in covenant language, is not a reaction to loss; it is a call for God's reversal. It is the sound of intercession when words alone fail.

The tearing of garments represents more than grief here in the story, it is in a sense, the symbolic renting of the veil between heaven and earth, where brokenness meets God's heart for man. God honors the fullness of what is offered through man's brokenness, especially in our sorrow.

"The Lord is near to the brokenhearted and saves those who are crushed in spirit." ~Psalm 34:18

It's no coincidence that there are more laments than songs of praise in the book of Psalms. The Psalter, which we often call the

Bible's songbook, is not primarily a record of joy, it is a testimony of the world's ache. It mirrors the human condition in all its fragility and longing. Through it, God is teaching us that lament is not the absence of worship, but rather, it is worship in its most honest form.

What should drive us away from the throne of grace through the weight of sorrow, grief, and pain then becomes, in truth, the very invitation for us to draw nearer. In heaven's language, sorrow is sacred.

It is not the rejection of faith but the raw material of intimacy itself.

This is what makes the story of Job so profound. Through all his lamentations, Job does not merely reveal the depth of his suffering, he reveals the depth of his knowing. His cries expose a man whose faith is not built on formulas, but forged through communion.

That is why his friends cannot understand him because they speak from theology and intellect, while Job speaks from encounter, and from intimacy.

But the truth remains, there can be no true intimacy without safety, and there can be no safety without trust. In other words, there is no intimacy in a relationship where one is not free to express the deepest and most sorrowful parts of their troubled heart.

God invites His people to trust Him enough to bring the truth of their pain, not a sanitized version, not the polished ritual, but the un-guarded heart. The very sorrows we try to hide become the offering laid upon the altar before the Lord who knows suffering all too well.

The world teaches us to approach God with composure, ritual, and control, but the reverence He desires is truth. So the true liturgy of the kingdom is not performance but presence.

He does not demand perfection of posture, but the honesty of your heart. For in the ashes, authenticity burns brightest, and the cry of lament becomes the very fragrance of worship itself.

The Awakening of Esther: From Comfort to Calling

"Then Esther's maids and her eunuchs came and told her, and the queen was deeply distressed." ~Esther 4:4

In some versions, the text says that Esther was *"seized by anguish."* (MEV) Either way, the Hebrew phrase implies not mere concern, but a visceral trembling; an inward shaking of the soul. It is the first crack in her insulated peace, the first tremor of awakening. For the first time, the cries outside her palace breach the silence within.

This is the mercy of God: to let comfort be interrupted by compassion.

Esther, who has until this point, lived veiled and guarded in luxury, now feels the reverberation of a unified cry and the voice of the very people she has concealed within herself.

She does what seems right in her limited understanding: she sends clothing to Mordecai to replace his sackcloth (v. 4).

But Mordecai refuses them.

This refusal is profoundly symbolic. Esther's instinct is to cover her kindred's grief, but Mordecai's calling is to embody it.

Her gesture represents the reflex of human nature: to fix pain rather than face it, and to silence our sorrow rather than enter it.

But Mordecai's rejection of comfort is, in my opinion, a deeply prophetic act. He will not let her soothe away the sound of lament, and he will not allow her to bypass the burden God intends her to bear.

In that moment, the kingdom of Persia meets the kingdom of heaven at the palace gate where comfort confronts conviction.

The Disruption

Esther's distress signals the beginning of internal disruption. Until now, she has navigated her role through grace, beauty, and wisdom, but not yet through spiritual burden. She has lived faithfully, but not yet prophetically.

Every calling has a moment like this: when your peace is disturbed by another's pain. When the cries of the afflicted reach you not as noise, but as summons.

Mordecai's lament becomes Esther's awakening. What began as public mourning becomes her invitation into deeper faith. God is teaching her what He teaches every intercessor, that compassion is not always sentiment, and the cries you cannot ignore are often the ones you are called to carry.

The Messenger Between Worlds

Most striking however, is that Esther's eunuch, Hathach, becomes the go-between and the messenger who carries words between a fasting man and a cloistered queen. Through him, the tension between faith and fear begins to unfold.

There is a beautiful irony here: communication between Mordecai and Esther depends entirely on an intermediary. The one who carries messages between the palace and the gate becomes a living symbol of intercession and the bridge be-tween lament and authority, and between grief and glory.

Through this exchange, Esther learns the true cost of calling. Mordecai does not ask her to speak as a queen, but to stand as a covenant daughter.

The Significance of Hathach

"Then Esther called for Hathach, one of the king's eunuchs, who had been appointed to attend her, and ordered him to go to Mordecai to learn what this was and why it was." ~ Esther 4:5

In the entire book of Esther, most palace officials and servants remain unnamed. We never learn the names of:

- The eunuchs who summon Vashti (Esther 1:10–12)
- The seven nobles who advise Ahasuerus (Esther 1:14)
- The keepers of the women who served in the harem (Esther 2:8)
- The scribes who record Haman's decree (Esther 3:12)

Yet Hathach is named, and only for this scene.

That narrative anomaly is deliberate. In Hebrew story-telling, when the author chooses to name a servant in a sea of anonymity, it signals narrative and theological importance.

Meaning and Implication

The name Hathach likely comes from a Persian root that possibly means "verily," "truthful," or "trustworthy."

It can also be related to the Hebrew concept of "cut" or "designate" — as in, set apart for a specific purpose. If that's the intended nuance, the name subtly underscores his uniquely appointed role in which

Hathach is the "set apart" one who carries truth between two worlds. In other words, he's more than just a messenger, he's the physical embodiment of faithful mediation.

The Mirror of Chapter 2

In Chapter 2, Esther finds favor with another eunuch, Hegai, the keeper of the women: *"And the young woman pleased him and won his favor, and he quickly provided her with her beauty treatments and her portion of food, and seven chosen maidens..."*
~Esther 2:9

Hegai prepared Esther for her first approach to the king, one of physical beauty, external favor, and positional elevation.

Now, Hathach prepares her for her second approach to the king, one of spiritual burden, inner transformation, and sacrificial inter-cession. Together, they represent the two stages of spiritual formation:

1. Outer Favor — The season of positioning (Hegai).
2. Inner Consecration — The season of calling (Hathach).

Between Two Realms

Eunuchs in ancient royal courts were not merely servants, they were liminal figures: trusted intermediaries who lived between access and absence.

They had the ear of the king, yet bore no lineage of their own. They symbolized devotion without inheritance and ser-vice without self-gain. So, in Esther's story, this becomes dee-ply theological.

Hathach lives between the king's court and the queen's chambers, yet is the bridge that connects the two worlds, just as Mordecai stands between the covenant people and the royal power at the gate.

Spiritually, Hathach mirrors the role of intercession itself, one who stands between realms, carrying the word of one kingdom to another.

He becomes a living symbol of the Holy Spirit's ministry:

"For the Spirit Himself intercedes for us with groanings too deep for words." ~Romans 8:26

Hathach moves silently between Esther and Mordecai, between the concealed queen and the lamenting gatekeeper, conveying revelation, urging response, and preparing obedience. In a book where God's name is absent, this quiet inter-mediary embodies His hidden communication.

So, Hathach's brief but pivotal appearance marks the turning point in Esther's transformation:

- Before him, Esther is passive and unaware.
- Through him, she begins to receive revelation.
- After him, she steps into purpose and authority.

CHAPTER FOUR

The Hesitation of Esther: When Favor Feels Distant

"All the king's servants and the people of the king's provinces know that if any man or woman goes to the king inside the inner court without being called, there is but one law—to be put to death, except the one to whom the king holds out the golden scepter so that he may live. But as for me, I have not been called to come in to the king these thirty days." ~Esther 4:11

Esther's response exposes the raw underside of royal life. She may wear a crown, but she does not command access. The favor that once elevated her now feels uncertain and suspended in silence.

For thirty days, the one who once basked in the king's favor has been shut out. The queen's hidden fear mirrors Israel's own anxiety in exile, asking the question: Has the King forgotten us?

The Fear Beneath the Faith

But Esther's confession is not rebellion, it's vulnerability. Before she risks her life for her people, she must first face her own sense of abandonment. She is saying, in essence: "How can I plead for others when I'm no longer sure of *my place* before the king?"

This moment reminds us that calling often meets us in the silence between what was and what will be. God often allows the distance so that faith must step forward without the assurance of visible favor.

Persian favor is fickle; it expires with the king's moods and whims. But covenant favor, by contrast, is eternal, and it rests on promise, not preference. The king's silence then becomes a parable:

- The throne of man can forget you after thirty days.
- But the throne of heaven engraves you on the palms of His hands. (Isaiah 49:16)

So, in essence, Esther's fear exposes the limits of human authority and the superiority of God's faithfulness.

> *"Can a woman forget her nursing child...? Even these may forget, yet I will not forget you." ~Isaiah 49:15*

The Contrast of the Two Thrones

At this point, two thrones stand in tension:

- The throne of Persia, where Esther's access is uncertain.
- The throne of heaven, where intercession is always heard.

Esther is caught between them, a symbol of every believer who must approach the greater King when all earthly favor has gone cold. Her courage will soon shift from confidence in human approval to trust in God's appointment.

The Thirty-Day Silence as a Test of Faith

In biblical symbolism, the number thirty can also mark transition or preparation for public commission:

- Joseph stood before Pharaoh at thirty (Genesis 41:46)
- David became king at thirty (2 Samuel 5:4)
- Jesus began His ministry at thirty (Luke 3:23)

Each "thirty" represents the threshold between obscurity and purpose. So, while Esther reads her thirty days as distance, heaven reads them as preparation. And before she stands in the royal courts, she must stand in faith alone.

When Favor Feels Lost

This moment of silence also tests the purity of Esther's obedience. Will she act only when she feels chosen? Or when she knows she is called?

The same question confronts us as believers: Do we move in obedience only when God's favor feels tangible, or when His voice stills every fear?

In the tension between silence and summons, Esther learns the essence of faith in that true favor is not the frequency of summons, but the constancy of calling.

The Turning Point: "For Such a Time as This"

"Do not think to yourself that in the king's palace you will escape any more than all the other Jews. For if you keep silent at this time, relief and deliverance will rise for the Jews from another place, but you and your father's house will perish. And who knows whether you have come to the kingdom for such a time as this?" ~ Esther 4:13–14

Mordecai's words are both a rebuke and a revelation for Esther. Up to this point, Esther's role has been passive: chosen, positioned, and prepared. But now her destiny demands a decision. Mordecai con-fronts her with two piercing truths:

- Her privilege will not protect her. *"Do not think you will escape..."*

  Mordecai reminds her that proximity to power is no refuge from spiritual accountability. The call of God transcends position and that no palace wall can insulate a soul from purpose.

- God's providence is not fragile. *"If you keep silent, deliverance will rise from another place..."* Mordecai's faith has matured. He's no longer pleading from a place of panic, he's now declaring from a place of conviction. His confidence in God's covenant plan is unshakable; deliverance *will* come. The only question is whether Esther will participate in it.

This is pure covenant theology: God's redemptive plan does not hinge on human compliance, but His invitations always carry eternal consequence.

"Who Knows?"

The phrase *"Who knows whether you have come to the kingdom for such a time as this?"* is one of Scripture's most artful examples of prophetic understatement.

The question that Mordecai is posing is not uncertainty, it's reverent awe. Mordecai is hinting that everything Esther endured (loss, exile, concealment, isolation, favor) was providential preparation for this very moment. In the Hebrew narrative, "Who knows?" (mi yodea) often introduces moments where human perception brushes against God's orchestration:

- *Joel 2:14* — *"Who knows whether He will turn and relent?"*
- *2 Samuel 12:22* — *"Who knows whether the Lord will be gracious to me?"*

The phrase holds mystery without doubt, and it acknow-ledges God's sovereignty that operates beyond human fore-sight. So Mordecai's statement is a masterpiece of both faith and hum-ility. In essence, he making a declarative statement through the question itself.

You may not have planned this moment, but God did.

The Role Reversal and the Rise of Spiritual Authority

"Go, gather all the Jews to be found in Susa, and hold a fast on my behalf... I and my young women will fast as you do. Then I will go to the king, though it is against the law, and if I perish, I perish."
~Esther 4:15–16

Until now, Mordecai has been the mentor and Esther the disciple. He has been the one who instructs and she obeys. But here the dynamic shifts dramatically in which the learner now becomes the leader.

Esther now gives the command.

So, where she once moved under covering, she now moves under commissioning. Her transformation is both literary and spiritual. This is the fruit of her hidden preparation and the spiri-tual refining through her obedience, waiting, and favor. God's process has graduated her from a passive vessel to an active inter-cessor.

Esther, the orphan girl who once hid her identity, now steps into spiritual motherhood over an entire people.

The Command to Fast

What's most remarkable about Esther's response is where she directs her focus. Her instinct is not first to assemble strategies, appeal to allies, or manipulate circumstances. In-stead, she goes straight to God.

> *"Go, gather all the Jews... and hold a fast for me."*
> *~Esther 4:16*

Esther has spent years learning how to move within the structures of an earthly kingdom. She knows the protocols, the danger, the unpredictable temper of the king. Yet when the decree of death falls, she does not turn to politics or persuasion, she turns to consecration. She recognizes that the problem they face is not political but spiritual.

No physical effort could redeem what only the Spirit of God could overturn. The empire's weapon was a decree written in ink, but its true power was spiritual in nature, root-ed in hatred, fear, and the ancient enmity between light and darkness.

Therefore, the only effective response must also be spiritual. In this moment, Esther transcends natural instinct and enters prophetic discernment. She understands what Mordecai could not yet articulate: that deliverance must be birthed through fasting before fighting, and through surrender before strategy.

This is what sets her apart and reveals the fruit of her hidden preparation. Every true deliverance begins in the invisible. So be-fore a decree can be reversed in the courts of men, it must first be confronted in the courts of heaven.

CHAPTER FOUR

The Symmetry of the Three Days

"Fast for me... do not eat or drink for three days, night or day."
Three days of darkness precede three days of deliverance. It is
a rhythm that repeats consistently throughout redemptive history:
- Jonah in the belly of the fish.
- Israel waiting between Passover and Exodus.
- Jesus in the tomb before resurrection.

The fasting of Esther's people anticipates the travail of Christ
in Gethsemane. Both are acts of substitutionary courage, standing
in the gap between decree and deliverance.

"If I Perish, I Perish"

This statement is not fatalism, it's actually surrender. It's the
language of those who have crossed over from being grip-ped fear
to being led by faith. Her words echo the faith of:
- Shadrach, Meshach, and Abednego: *"But if not, we will not
  bow." (Daniel 3:18)*
- Jesus in Gethsemane: *"Not my will, but Yours be done." (Luke
  22:42)*

Here Esther passes from self-preservation to self-offering.

In that moment, she becomes more than a queen, she becomes
an intercessor, priest, and a vessel of redemption.

The Final Line: Mordecai's Obedience

*"So Mordecai went away and did exactly as Esther com-
manded him." ~Esther 4:17*

This closing verse seals the role reversal for this chapter.

The one who once directed now willingly obeys. The man who stood in sackcloth now moves under the authority of the woman he once mentored. It is a portrait of spiritual order through humility which shows us that when obedience meets alignment, heaven moves. The last line reads almost quietly, but it's thunder in disguise. So the decree of fasting has gone out, and the war has shifted into the spiritual realm.

CHAPTER FOUR

CLOSING REMARKS

So often, we look at our circumstances as either meaningless to our purpose or the very unraveling of it altogether. And when we search for God in the midst of it, we find our-selves wondering where He is, or why He would allow such things to happen.

We carry these grand ideas of how our lives should unfold, yet what we thought would happen often crumbles before our eyes. Worse still, the prayers we've carried for years can begin to feel like distant echoes of disillusioned dreams. The promises we once clung to seem buried beneath the ruins of disappointment, and one heartbreak after another that never seems to end.

But as neither Mordecai nor Esther could have foreseen, what looked like the end of their story became the beginning of God's. Their ruin became the very soil of redemption.

Despite the chaos and the silence of God, they turned their attention to the only course of action worthy of their effort—their appeal to the heart of the One who rules over all things, including ruin itself. They knew His heart was one that hears the cries of His people. And that knowledge compelled them to press deeper into the silence until their voices reached heaven.

Rather than trusting in themselves to turn the tide of their fate, they sought the One who holds fate itself in His hands. And as they pressed into that silence, they began to recognize that God had been moving all along from the very beginning.

So often we ask God to *give* us faith in times of need, not realizing that those very moments of need are the testing grounds where faith itself is *cultivated*.

REFLECTION & DISCUSSION

1. When comfort becomes insulation rather than security, the cries outside our walls grow faint.

   Where has comfort kept you from hearing the ache God intends you to carry? What small act of re-engagement—listening, fasting, visiting, etc.—could reopen your ears without hardening your heart?

2. If sorrow is the raw material of intimacy, then our pain becomes the meeting place between heaven and earth.

   What sorrow have you been polishing, keeping distant, or hiding behind composure? What would it look like to lay that grief bare before God as your truest form of worship?

3. Mordecai's lament became Esther's awakening, a reminder that another's anguish is often our summons.

   Whose pain has God placed near you, not to fix, but to feel and carry before Him? What cry have you been hearing that might actually be your calling?

4. "For such a time as this" is not just a statement of chance.

    Looking back, what moments of concealment, loss, or delay
    might have been God's preparation for the place you stand in
    now?

5. Fasting was Esther's first act of war; the invisible rebellion that
    shifted an empire.

    What situation in your life cannot be solved through strategy
    but only through surrender? How might God be calling you
    to fast, not just from food, but from self-reliance?

CHAPTER FIVE

The Fruit of Faith

On the third day, Esther put on her royal apparel and positioned herself in the king's palace courtyard so that she would be directly in line with the part of the king's throne room where the king sat, facing the entrance of the room on his royal throne in the royal hall.

~Esther 5:1

Faith Without Answer

The fifth chapter of Esther opens with stillness after the storm. The decree has gone forth, the fast has ended, and all of heaven seems silent. It appears that Esther does not receive a direct answer from the fast. The text gives no revelation, no direct response from God, and no visible sign of deliverance. Instead, she emerges from her three days of fasting not with certainty, but rather, the crushing weight of silence that she was hoping to break through.

The Loneliness of the Calling

She also no longer receives counsel from her servants, as advice had often appeared throughout the story whenever it was prompted. Here, Esther is acting of her own volition. For the first time, she stands entirely on her own, with nothing left to rely on but her faith in the One who can save her and her people.

Perhaps she had hoped for a direct answer — a word of clarity or strategy — to emerge from the fast. Yet, consistent with the pattern of this book, there is no mention of prayer and therefore no explicit response from God.

The narrative is told from a human perspective entirely, and yet this becomes the most spiritual movement in the story thus far. God has not overtly spoken, yet the faith she needed was granted, not in the way she expected, but through the quiet mercy that works even in fear.

This, in essence, becomes the very ground by which her submission without clarity continues to cultivate faith even when she feels it is absent. From everything she has been provisioned with since the beginning of her story until now, this moment marks a stark contrast: Esther has shifted from dependence on man to dependence fully on God alone.

We often hold an idealized picture of what faith should look like, but here, faith is simply "just enough", as it most often is. And that "just enough" grants us favor in the eyes of the King far beyond what we could ever hope for.

It reminds us that trembling faith is still real faith. Elijah once stood in that same silence (1 Kings 19), where the Lord was not in the wind, nor the fire, nor the earthquake, but in the still small voice that followed.

Finding Favor from the Throne

Here, the text draws us into the quiet tension of Esther's decision, the moment she chooses to move forward despite the silence. The simple act of dressing herself in royal garments is both haunting and human: haunting, because she does so beneath the weight of uncertainty; human, because it shows faith rising from the tension between fear and obedience.

Perhaps she cannot even bring herself to speak as she prepares for what feels like her own death sentence. She still does not know whether the king will receive her or reject her. And though she adorns herself in royal robes, those garments cannot conceal the trembling fear within.

Yet still, she presses on.

She steps into the courtyard, just outside the king's throne room. Notice that she does not immediately approach him. Instead, she positions herself within view, just close enough to be seen, yet distant enough to remain reverent.

If she can only be seen, perhaps she will know if favor still remains.

So, she approaches not in perfection but in weakness, risking rejection, and that very risk becomes the doorway to favor. This is faith expressed not through bold stride but through measured nearness; a kind of courage that dares to stand within sight of the throne, even when the outcome is uncertain. Esther does not rush in with the confidence of conquest; she simply positions herself close enough to be seen. That, in itself, is faith.

The contrast with "coming boldly to the throne of grace" (Hebrews 4:16) forms a powerful bridge between Esther's court and the believer's access to God through Christ. Her trembling posture before the king's scepter mirrors our own before the throne of heaven, yet the difference is striking.

Under the old covenant, Esther's boldness could reach only as far as proximity; under the new, our boldness leads to communion. Christ Himself has extended the golden scepter once and for all.

And "boldly" does not mean without fear. It means bringing the whole self—fear, weakness, uncertainty, and all—into His presence without disguise. Esther's boldness is not brash confidence but sacred dependence, the collision of reverence and trust in a single act of faith.

Thus, this opening verse of chapter 5 does more than move the story forward, it draws every believer into that same tension: the ache of fasting, praying, and hearing nothing. It is the moment where faith either falters or deepens.

What happens when we seek God through prayer and fasting, and He remains silent? When no sign comes, no voice speaks, and yet we must still decide whether to move forward?

That is where true faith is cultivated, within the quiet courage to stand, trusting that favor still waits on the other side of the silence.

Faith as the Turning Point

It is also no coincidence that Chapter 5 becomes the center stage of Esther's story, the moment where the tide be-gins to turn, and all of it revolves around faith.

In Hebrew storytelling, the middle of a book often holds its theological heart. Esther 5 stands as the hinge of reversal, both in plot and in meaning. Everything before it descends into decree, despair, and fasting; everything after it rises into deliverance, exposure, and redemption.

At the midpoint of a book where God's name is never spoken, faith emerges as the unseen axis on which everything turns. Faith becomes the hinge that turns hiddenness into revelation. And grace blooms in the middle, not at the beginning or the end, but in the space between.

Think about the sequence:

- Chapters 1–4: Human power, decrees, fear, hiddenness.
- Chapter 5: Faith steps forward in silence.
- Chapters 6–10: Divine reversal, justice, exaltation, peace.

  Faith, then, is the turning key.

The moment Esther steps into that courtyard—terrified yet trusting—the entire cosmic tide begins to shift. It is as though God waits for faith's movement before history itself pivots.

The fact that this happens in the middle chapter is not random; it is symbolic of faith standing as the very center point between despair and deliverance. Structurally, it mirrors the hidden pattern of grace.

Grace often meets us in the middle:

- The middle of the storm (Mark 6:47–50).
- The middle cross at Calvary.
- The middle of history itself—Christ's incarnation dividing time.

And so, Chapter 5 sits at the "middle cross" of Esther, and the place where silence meets surrender, and surrender meets favor.

Thematically, it reflects the hidden God becoming revealed through faith. Up to this point, God has been veiled; after this, His providence unfolds visibly through Haman's fall and Mordecai's rise.

Chapter 5, then, is the threshold between concealment and rev-elation, and the moment where grace begins to lift the veil. Faith becomes the door through which the hidden God steps once again into human history. And it is here that hu-man weakness becomes the vessel through which faith moves and God's strength is revealed.

The Raised Scepter: Favor Extended

So much to Esther's relief, the king raises his golden scepter and summons her in. It is the long-awaited break in the silence, or the pause between death and deliverance. One can almost feel the weight of despair lift from her shoulders as she steps forward and reaches for the scepter, grasping it as though it were her very life-line.

The raised scepter stands as both literal mercy and symbolic salvation, and a visible sign that death has passed her by.

In this simple gesture, the text invites us to witness the mercy of God reflected through human authority. For though the favor of kings may waver, the favor of God remains stead-fast. What is uncertain in the eyes of men is unshakable in the heart of God.

The scepter extended before Esther becomes a mirror of God's grace and an image of the greater invitation extended to every believer.

"Let us therefore come boldly unto the throne of grace..."
~Hebrews 4:16

The earthly king offers Esther half his kingdom while the heavenly King offers His fullness. One gestures toward generosity, the other embodies it completely.

Thus, Esther's approach to the throne is not merely an act of courage, it is a foreshadowing of grace, a glimpse of the God's own exchange that would later be fulfilled through Christ Himself.

This moment also magnifies God's extravagant generosity following mercy. His favor not only spares, but it re-wards.

"He lavished grace upon us" ~Ephesians 1:8

The earthly king's overabundance becomes a reflection of God's far greater abundance, and the God who not only re-stores what was feared lost but multiplies it instead.

"Now to Him who is able to do immeasurably more than all we ask or imagine..." ~Ephesians 3:20

Through this single act of the king, Esther's favor becomes more than political acceptance, it becomes a foreshadowing of adoption and inheritance, a glimpse of the believer's own standing before the true King who reigns forever.

The Delay of Faith

Having received the king's favor, Esther does not immediately voice her request. Instead, she invites the king and Haman to a banquet. The text offers no explicit reason for her delay, and interpreters have long debated her motives. Some see a deliberate strategy through a calculated plan to stir the king's curiosity and strengthen her influence. Others see hesitation born from a desire to wait for clearer confirmation.

But perhaps both are true. For faith often walks the narrow line between planning and dependence. What is clear is that Esther's courage continues to grow, even in the presence of uncertainty.

Only days before, she had doubted whether the king even remembered her. Now, she stands before him, received with favor and offered more than she could have imagined. Such a reversal— so swift and so unexpected—would have over-whelmed any heart still recovering from fear. Her pause, then, is not evidence of unbelief, but the natural process of faith in motion. It reminds us that grace often appears in places where guilt and doubt expect rejection.

And notice how Esther responds to that grace—not with passivity, but with further movement. Her faith takes another step forward. God's favor, in her case, becomes not an end-point, but a launching point for obedience.

This moment also exposes the honesty of the human condition, where Esther stands suspended between mercy and fear, processing both at once.

The First Banquet

When the first banquet arrives, Esther finds herself seated across from both her husband and her enemy. Only three days earlier, she had first heard of Haman's decree. Now she must look into the face of the man who ordered her people's destruction. The text does not tell us that her fear vanished, and rightly so. For true faith does not silence fear; it learns to walk in its company.

This shift from grace to inner conflict mirrors the believer's own oscillation between faith and fear. So, the banquet becomes a silent battlefield of the spirit.

And here, the reader is invited to notice the deep irony of the scene: the table of favor also hosts the architect of destruction. Deliverance, it seems, often unfolds in the very presence of danger.

"You prepare a table before me in the presence of my enemies."
~Psalm 23:5

This scene also reveals the mystery of faith's timing. What looks like delay is often God's preparation. Sometimes, what feels like hesitation is actually providence unfolding at a pace through which grace has pre-pared the way.

"The Lord will fight for you; you need only to be still."
~Exodus 14:14

Trembling Obedience

Esther is not yet fearless, nor is she fully composed. She hesitates, yet she remains faithful. Through this, we see that God does not demand perfect boldness, only obedient movement. What He asks for is not the roar of confidence, but the quiet step of trust.

This same pattern appears in the story of Gideon. When the angel of the Lord called him a *"mighty warrior,"* Gideon looked around in disbelief, hiding from the very battle he was called to fight (Judges 6:12–15). Yet God saw beyond Gideon's fear, just as He saw beyond Esther's trembling. Where man sees limitation, God sees the seed of redemption. Where we see weakness, He sees a vessel ready for His strength (2 Corinthians 12:9).

The very things we assume disqualify us often become the material through which God displays His glory. This is the paradox of grace, where disqualification becomes qualification. Even the smallest, most hesitant act of obedience—the faint movement of faith that barely steps into the court-yard—is counted as boldness in God's eyes. For He measures courage not by the absence of fear, but by the willingness to move through it.

Esther's approach to the throne reminds us that grace does not demand perfection before it extends favor. That sing step toward obedience is itself an act of worship. And when faith moves, however quietly, heaven moves with it. Yet even as grace steadies Esther, pride elsewhere begins to unravel.

Mordecai's Stillness and Haman's Decay

The story now shifts, drawing a sharp contrast between two hearts shaped at two very different tables; one fed by fasting, the other by feasting.

Haman leaves the royal banquet *"joyful and glad of heart,"* basking in the favor of both the king and queen. Yet his joy is short-lived. It is the kind of joy that burns bright for a moment and dies in the wake of offense. His gladness is not born of peace, but of pride, and not of faith, but of flattery.

108

For Haman, happiness lives and dies in the gaze of others. His sense of worth depends entirely on being seen, admired, and obeyed. But when he steps outside the palace and sees Mordecai at the gate standing unmoved, his entire illusion of control begins to unravel.

The very sight of Mordecai's calm pierces through his fragile joy. What was laughter moments before curdles into wrath. Such is the volatility of pride, and how quickly joy rooted in self collapses when con-fronted by a peace it cannot command.

And in that moment, Haman's joy is exposed for what it truly is: a hollow crown that cannot survive contradiction.

Mordecai at the Gate

In contrast, Mordecai's peace stands in quiet defiance of everything Haman represents. The man who once tore his robes in anguish now stands at the same gate, clothed not in mourning, but in resolve. The fast has changed him. His silence is no longer grief, it has become strength. The very place that once witnessed his despair now becomes the ground of his steadfast faith.

He stands where he has always stood, yet something in him is profoundly different. Outwardly, nothing has changed, but inwardly, everything has. The gate was once a symbol of helplessness, but has now become a threshold of authority.

Mordecai stands firm not because he is fearless, but because he has learned to fear rightly. He fears God; therefore, he fears no man (Matthew 10:28). Such is the kind of faith that remains unmoved even in the face of death.

This is what Paul later describes in Ephesians 6: *"Having done all, to stand."* Mordecai's stand is not stubbornness, it is spiritual warfare in stillness. He does not shout, argue, or strive; he simply stands. And in doing so, he unsettles Haman's empire. So, his peace becomes his protest, and his calm be-comes his weapon. For true faith does not always shout; sometimes, it simply refuses to flinch.

The Corrosion of Pride

While Esther and Mordecai emerge from fasting transformed by humility, Haman emerges from feasting poisoned by pride. The contrast could not be sharper; one is emptied and strengthened; the other is filled and hollowed.

This chapter then reveals two harvests: the fruit of faith and the fruit of arrogance. Haman's joy lasts only as long as his ego is fed, and the moment someone refuses him reverence, his joy dies of hunger. He has tasted the sweetness of honor and cannot bear the bitterness of defiance.

The text gives us a fleeting image of triumph, but it fades as quickly as it appears, just as the wicked in Psalm 73, whose prosperity vanishes like smoke. A heart swollen by pride cannot stand the sight of peace it cannot control. And Mordecai's stillness becomes the mirror reflecting Haman's emptiness.

The more Mordecai stands still, the louder Haman's unrest grows. That is the torment of the wicked, where the peace of the righteous becomes their judgment.

"The wicked flee when no one pursues, but the righteous are bold as a lion." ~Proverbs 28:1

Mordecai's boldness, therefore, is not noise or aggression; it is the unshakable composure of a man who knows whom he serves. And as Isaiah writes, "There is no peace... for the wicked" (Isaiah 48:22).

So, Haman, cloaked in royal favor, becomes the most tormented man in the empire, while Mordecai, still bearing the mark of his fast, remains the most at peace.

The Agony of Unyielded Pride

"Nevertheless, Haman restrained himself, and when he came to his home, he sent for his friends and for his wife Zeresh." ~Esther 5:10

Haman returns home filled with indignation, gathering his audience to rehearse his glory. He lists his riches, sons, promotions, and honors, as though reciting them could silence the echo of Mordecai's defiance. But his efforts fail.

The higher he lifts his achievements, the lower his peace descends.

And his confession breaks forth like the cry of an unhealed soul: *"Yet all this avails me nothing, so long as I see Mordecai the Jew sitting at the king's gate." (Esther 5:13)*

It is the essence of pride laid bare, where everything is meaningless until everything bows. That is the curse of arrogance

111

in which it cannot rest until every knee bends, not to God, but to itself. Haman's hatred reveals a deeper spiritual truth: the wicked are never content with influence; they crave worship. And when righteousness refuses to yield, that refusal becomes their torment.

Zeresh: The Voice That Builds the Gallows

When Haman returns home seething with fury, the narrative shifts to the voice behind the man. He gathers his friends and his wife, Zeresh, to boast of his glory and lament his grievance, and it is her counsel he heeds.

This moment is interesting when we remember how the book began with another queen, Vashti, whose defiance cost her the throne. Vashti lost her voice through resistance where-as Zeresh wields hers through manipulation. And between these two women, Esther rises with a voice guided not by pride, but by restraint and intercession.

Zeresh, in contrast, becomes the embodiment of corrupted counsel. She is not merely Haman's wife; she is the echo of pride made audible. Her words carry the same venom that fuels her husband's ego, and through them, she seals both their fates.

"Let a gallows fifty cubits high be made..." ~Esther 5:14

In one sentence, Zeresh speaks death into motion. What she builds for another becomes the very structure of her own undoing. It is not coincidence, it is irony. The counsel of pride always builds its own gallows.

The Counterpart of Esther

Zeresh stands as Esther's shadow; a feminine counterpart to pride and the spiritual antithesis of intercession. Both women influence kings. Both speak into power. But one speaks life through submission, while the other speaks death through manipulation.

Where Esther commands a fast, Zeresh commands construction.

Where one humbles herself before the throne, the other exalts herself through counsel.

Through this contrast, the battlefield of Chapter 5 widens. The true conflict is not fought with swords, but with words. Both women command action, yet one aligns with heaven, and the other with the kingdom of darkness. This is the hidden warfare of influence, and proof that voices, not just armies, shape the outcome of spiritual wars.

The Jezebel Pattern

Zeresh's counsel recalls another woman in Scripture: Jezebel (1 Kings 21:1–16). Both urged their husbands toward violence in the name of pride. Both manipulated authority to serve their own ambitions. And both brought destruction upon their own households.

Scripture often reveals truth through repetition, and this pattern—where pride speaks through persuasion—marks Zeresh as more than a passive character. She becomes a spiritual type. Her voice represents the counterfeit of godly counsel, and an echo of demonic persuasion operating through influence in high places.

Zeresh is, in essence, Jezebel reborn in Persia, speaking deceit with the confidence of revelation.

Esther's Feminine Theology

Without Zeresh, the book's feminine theology would remain incomplete. Each of the three women—Vashti, Esther, and Zeresh—embodies a dimension of influence, forming together a spiritual mirror of feminine power and responsibility.

- Vashti reveals the cost of refusal without reverence.
- Esther reveals the sanctified voice of obedience through surrender
- Zeresh reveals the corruption of counsel and the anti-voice of intercession.

Through them, the book of Esther unveils the moral geometry of influence, and the power of a woman's voice to shape more than just their own household.

Where Esther's holiness shines brighter, Zeresh's corruption darkens the scene. Together, they reveal that a wo-man's influence, whether yielded to God or corrupted by self, can alter the fate of kingdoms.

The Feminine Battle Beneath the Surface

While the men of the story war through decrees, rank, and status, the women war through influence, words, and hidden authority. And here, in the closing movement of Chapter 5, two kinds of spiritual motherhood emerge:

- One that births deliverance (Esther).
- One that births destruction (Zeresh).

This typology at its deepest level, is Eve's divided legacy replaying through history once more. Through Esther, faith is birthed in intercession. Through Zeresh, pride is birthed in counsel. And between the two, the narrative shifts in which two women speak, and heaven answers only one.

The Unfolding Tension

As the chapter closes, Zeresh's words still hang in the air—"Build the gallows." They linger like a curse spoken over her own household.

Even as Esther's faith begins to bloom in the king's court, darkness ripens in Haman's home. The text allows both to grow in parallel—the obedience of faith and the rebellion of pride—until their collision reveals God's justice.

This is spiritual tension by design: grace and pride growing side by side, each maturing toward its appointed end. Zeresh's voice becomes the final note of contrast, and a chilling reminder that the book of Esther is not merely about decrees and destiny, but about counsel and consequence.

And as Haman sets out to build his gallows, he does not yet realize that he is constructing the very instrument of his own ruin.

Closing Remarks

Mordecai and Esther both made a choice that day. Faith, at its heart, is always a choice and a yielding of the soul in submission. Each of us must decide who will reign upon the throne of our hearts: will it be fear or trust, doubt or worship?

We either lay ourselves upon the altar of fear, or upon the altar of faith. And faith, therefore transforms us into the likeness of its object. It grows within us, shaping us inwardly and outwardly until our hearts mirror what we trust most.

At the opening of this chapter, Esther's faith is only beginning to take root. She lingers in the courtyard, gripped by fear, and uncertain, waiting to see if favor remains. Mordecai, however, stands unmoved. His roots have grown deep. The fast has not weakened him; it has fortified him. His faith had already been settled when he called Esther to courage. The fast did not birth belief but strengthened what was already alive.

These are two different expressions of faith, where one is sprouting, and the other is steadfast, yet both are alive and pleasing to God. So, faith is not measured by maturity, but by its motion. Esther's step forward and Mordecai's stillness both display the same fruit of faith. And that same rooted faith, which enables one to move and the other to remain unmoved, becomes the very thing that agitates the heart of the wicked.

Mordecai's stillness becomes Haman's torment.

So, it is not more faith that we need, as God has already given each of us a measure sufficient for every trial. And the call is not to strive for greater faith, but to cultivate the faith already given, which is to remain deeply rooted in Christ.

For it is not human effort that lifts us upward, but surrender that allows us to fall freely into the arms of grace. And that grace is what carries us to the very end. Paul spoke of running his race well, not because of his strength, but because grace carried him across the finish line.

So, this chapter becomes the subtle revealing of faith's fruit, and though it is never named outright, it is the silent current moving through every scene.

What appears as ordinary life is the stage upon which faith, humility, and pride unfold together. Faith takes the center, not only transforming Esther and Mordecai, but exposing the decay of Haman and his household.

And here lies the paradox at the heart of the chapter: Faith without answer is still faith that moves heaven.

It is the kind of faith that does not demand proof before it obeys, but faith that acts beneath silence rather than above it. This is where Job meets Hebrews 11, which painted faith not as triumphalism, but as trembling obedience.

And yet, faith is not effort, it is rest.

This is what Jesus meant when He said, *"Abide in Me, and I in you... for apart from Me you can do nothing."*

The abiding itself is the work of faith, and the trust that grace will carry what obedience begins. And that is why He also said,

"My yoke is easy, and My burden is light." For in Him, even the trembling stand still becomes rest.

But this rest is not natural to the human heart. Esther's silence before the throne feels unnatural because everything in the flesh cries out to preserve, to fix, and to control. Her restraint becomes spiritual violence against the flesh, and it is there, in that stillness, that her transformation begins.

True faith does not conquer fear through force; it crucifies self-reliance through surrender. To abide, then, is not a passive act. It is the hardest rest a soul can learn, the rest that kills control.

Dependence feels unnatural because it is. Yet it is precisely there, in the tension between fear and trust, that faith begins to breathe. We are not faithless because dependence feels uncomfortable; it is in that discomfort that faith is made real. So, faith does not conquer fear by denying it, it passes through fear by yielding to grace.

And this is the beauty of Christ's invitation: He does not ask us to escape our humanity to find Him. Instead, He enters it with us. He invites the fearfulness, the doubt, and the ache. The most visceral parts of our humanity do not repel His grace; they become the very ground upon which grace grows.

Too often we treat our frailty as disqualification before the throne, but in truth, it becomes the offering itself. But grace does not bypass the human condition, it sanctifies it.

For Esther, that grace looked like trembling in fear yet moving forward anyway. For us, it looks like bringing the unedited, unpolished parts of ourselves before the throne instead of hiding them.

And grace is not a spiritual commodity to be acquired; it is Christ Himself drawing near in the very moment we sur-render.

When Esther stepped into the courtyard, she was not walking toward an abstract hope but toward the unseen presence of the true King, the One who had already extended His scepter long before the earthly king raised his own.

Faith, then, grants us not the strength to hold tighter, but the courage to fall freely into the arms of grace, for Christ is the fullness of grace itself. And this fall is not failure, but surrender. Surrender that produces the outcome not of control or certainty, but of communion with the One who holds the scepter.

Reflection and Discussion

1. Esther emerged from fasting into a silence that spoke louder than words. There was no voice, and no sign, only the call to step forward without assurance.

   In the silence of your own waiting, what kind of faith is being formed within you?

2. Esther's faith moved while Mordecai's faith remained, yet both were obedient. One acted, while the other abided.

   In your current season, which form of obedience reflects true trust, motion or stillness?

3. Esther's restraint before the throne was not hesitation, but surrender, an act of spiritual violence against her own instinct to control.

   What areas of your life have you called "caution," when in truth they were fear resisting faith?

4. Haman's joy was fragile because it was rooted in being seen. The moment one man refused to bow, his peace collapsed. Pride always feeds on validation and starves without it.

Where has your contentment become dependent on being noticed by man rather than being known by God?

5. Zeresh urged her husband toward destruction under the guise of control, while Esther waited in stillness under the posture of surrender. Both women spoke into power, yet only one aligned with God.

    When crisis arises, whose voice are you echoing; the one that builds the gallows, or the one that moves heaven?

CHAPTER SIX

The King Remembers

During that night the king could not sleep, so he ordered that the book of memorable acts (the chronicles) be brought, and they were read before the king. ~Esther 6:1

The Sleepless King

The opening of chapter six unfolds at the perfect intersection of God's timing and human scheming. Haman plots in the night, eager to secure Mordecai's death, while at that same hour, the king lies awake, restless, and unable to sleep.

And once again, the story draws our attention to God's hand moving simultaneously with the council of evil. It is a reminder that heaven's plans run parallel to the schemes of darkness, not in reaction to them, but in preemptive sovereignty. As Joseph said to his brothers in Genesis 50:20, *"You meant it for evil, but God meant it for good."*

This moment also echoes Psalm 2, where *"the nations plot in vain,"* yet *"He who sits in the heavens laughs."* The writer of Esther is showing us that even as men conspire in pride, God is already at work to turn their designs inside out. His timing is not delayed; it is deliberate.

When the text says, *"That night the king could not sleep,"* it forms a poetic parallel between the sleepless king of Persia and the ever-watchful King of Heaven.

"He who keeps Israel neither slumbers nor sleeps." ~ Psalm 121:4

The king's insomnia becomes a faint reflection and a shadow of the One who never closes His eyes on His people. Ahasuerus tosses and turns, but God watches and governs. Only one truly keeps His covenant.

The Book of Chronicles

In his restlessness, the king calls for the *book of chronicles* to be read aloud. What follows is not random; it's providence disguised as routine.

The king's record of remembrance becomes a typological reflection of the *Book of Life* itself, and a picture of God's memory that distinguishes between what is forgotten and what is forever written. Scripture tells us that God, unlike men, *"forgets iniquity and remembers righteousness" (Isaiah 43:25; Hebrews 10:17).* In the same way, the chronicles of the king serve as a literary mirror in which the deeds of faithfulness are recorded while acts of betrayal fade into obscurity.

So, this moment becomes more than a royal discovery, it becomes a portrait of justification. Mordecai's remembrance is not just an overdue honor; it is symbolic of God's principle of spiritual memory: to remember the righteous, not because they are flawless, but because they are faithful.

"It was counted to him [Abraham] for righteousness."
~Romans 4:3

"Those who feared the Lord spoke with one another, and the Lord listened and heard; a book of remembrance was written before Him for those who feared His name." ~ Malachi 3:16

Together these passages reveal a unique pattern in which faith is counted for righteousness and righteousness is remembered forever.

This same principle is echoed in Hebrews, where Lot—though flawed and hesitant—is still remembered as righteous (Hebrews 11:7). God's redemptive memory does not white-wash imperfection; it re-defines it through covenant grace.

So, as the king's servant reads of Mordecai's long-forgot-ten act of loyalty, we are reminded that nothing done in faith ever escapes the gaze of heaven. And what man forgets, God remembers. What seems buried beneath time's silence, grace brings back to light.

The Keepers of the Door

The text then recalls two names—Bigthana and Teresh—the eunuchs who conspired against the king. Their names are not throw-away details. The author includes them intentionally, not as historical trivia, but as moral contrasts.

These men were *keepers of the door*, stationed at the threshold of access to the throne. Mordecai, too, had been *"seated at the king's gate,"* positioned at another threshold—the dividing line between the inner court and the outer world.

Both stood close to power, but their postures could not be more different: one sought betrayal, the other preservation. The text invites us to see the contrast in which those who are entrusted with proximity to authority can either use that nearness to conspire against it or to guard it. Mordecai stands as the faithful gatekeeper and loyal where others faltered. This pattern of contrast with the eunuchs continues through-out the book:

- In chapter 2, the eunuch serves Esther, preparing her for favor.
- In chapter 4, Hathach becomes a messenger of obedience between Mordecai and Esther.
- In chapter 6, Bigthana and Teresh embody corruption and betrayal.

Through these shifting roles, the author subtly exposes the instability of human institutions. Even those closest to the throne of men are prone to treachery, but those who stand near the throne of God remain steadfast.

Mordecai's faithfulness at the gate becomes a silent re-buke to every corrupted system of man's making, and a reminder that God's purposes move forward through those who remain stead-fast, even when unseen.

Mordecai Remembered

The king, who until now has been marked by indulgence and moral blindness, suddenly acts with an uncharacteristic sense of justice. Upon realizing that nothing had been done to honor Mordecai for saving his life, he seeks to make it right. It is one of the few commendable moments we see from him in the entire story, and an earthly glimpse of a higher throne breaking into human affairs.

Though Xerxes remains unaware, his decision mirrors the justice of God. Even through imperfect rulers, the Lord displays His ability to accomplish righteousness on behalf of His people. The king's remembrance becomes the hinge of supernatural timing, not a coincidence, but God's sovereignty set into motion at the appointed hour.

"The vision is yet for an appointed time... though it tarry, wait for it." ~Habakkuk 2:3

Mordecai's reward was not denied, it was only delayed until the moment it would bring down Haman's pride. God's timing is never neglect; it is precision. What seems forgotten in the courts of men is never unrecorded in the courts of heaven. So Faithfulness may be over-looked for a season, but in the Kingdom, delay does not mean denial.

The Irony of Timing: Two Men, Two Motives

At the very hour the king remembers Mordecai, Haman cannot rest. He has just received the counsel of his wife and friends, urging him to build the gallows for Mordecai's execution. Blinded by obsession, he rushes to the palace to secure the king's permission.

This is where irony saturates the story. The same night one man is stirred toward honor, another is stirred toward murder. The sleepless king and the restless enemy move in parallel, each unaware that their steps are being choreographed by God's hands.

It's a contrast that exposes the split paths of destiny with God's purpose on one side, and demonic impulse on the other. While the king's insomnia opens the door to remembrance, Haman's impatience drives him toward ruin.

His hatred has become more than political, it is spiritual. The spirit of Amalek moves through him, a rage against the covenant line that refuses to bow. And just as Proverbs 16:18 warns, *"Pride goes before destruction,"* and Haman's arrogance becomes the very instrument of his undoing.

So, God doesn't need to intervene with thunder or fire; He simply lets pride hurry its own destruction.

Haman's Access and Influence

That Haman could approach the king's inner court at such an hour reveals the depth of his privilege. The Persian palace was one of the most heavily guarded institutions in the ancient world, even Esther risked death to enter unsummoned (Esther 4:11). Yet Haman walks in freely before dawn.

This detail tells us much:

- He likely had standing clearance to approach the king at will.

- He was part of the inner political circle, trusted among those who advised the throne.
- His presence had become so normalized that no guard questioned his approach.

This was not the behavior of a man who had only recently gained favor. It was the confidence of someone long embedded in power, and a man whose influence stretched across years of political advancement.

A History of Favor and Pride

Haman's promotion back in Esther 3:1 — *"After these things King Ahasuerus promoted Haman..."* — was not a random event. The phrase *"after these things"* suggests a gap of time between Esther's coronation and this moment, likely covering the years after Xerxes' failed Greek campaign.

When the king returned defeated and humiliated, he sought stability and loyalty in his administration. Haman, politically shrewd and already established, was the perfect candidate to elevate. Scholars note that his title, *"Haman the Agagite,"* is paired with *"the king advanced him and set his seat above all princes,"* implying that he surpassed even long-serving nobles.

This means Haman wasn't new to the court. He had likely witnessed Vashti's fall, Esther's rise, and the entire reordering of the royal household. He was the kind of man who knew how to survive transitions, was ambitious, calculating, and always near the center of power.

When he later boasts in Esther 5:11 of *"the glory of his riches, the multitude of his children, and all the ways the king had promoted him,"* he isn't exaggerating. He's rehearsing a lifetime of achievement. His wealth, his sons, and his honors mark him as one of the most powerful men in the empire.

This makes Mordecai's defiance far more humiliating. It wasn't merely one man refusing another; it was a public act of resistance before the royal court, and a refusal to bow that pierced Haman's pride to its core.

Providence at Work in the Irony

Notice how everything turns in this chapter in which humiliation becomes honor, plotting becomes proclamation, and pride becomes the unwilling servant of grace. The timing is almost comedic in its perfection: as Haman enters the court to request permission to execute Mordecai, the king calls for whoever happens to be present to help him honor the man who saved his life.

"The wicked plots against the righteous... but the Lord laughs at him, for He sees that his day is coming." ~Psalm 37:12–13

God uses Haman's impatience to deliver him into His own plan. The very ambition that drives him to act prematurely becomes the mechanism of reversal.

"A man plans his way, but the Lord directs his steps."
~ Proverbs 16:9

Both the king and Haman are blind to what's really happening. One seeks to reward, the other to destroy, yet both are unknowingly serving the same purpose.

Everyone who exalts himself will be humbled, and he who humbles himself will be exalted." ~ Luke 14:11

Mordecai never sought recognition, yet honor came for him anyway. Haman grasped for glory, and humiliation came in its place. So, the hands of men may write their plans, but the pen still belongs to God.

Haman Summoned

As the king calls Haman into the court, unaware of his intent, he asks a question that will seal Haman's fate: *"What shall be done for the man whom the king delights to honor?" ~Esther 6:6*

Without hesitation, Haman describes the very exaltation he craves for himself, a public display of power, glory, and recognition. In doing so, he writes the script for his own humiliation. So, what he intends as self-promotion becomes the framework for irony.

A Foreshadowing of Christ's Exaltation

In this scene, Haman's prescribed pageantry becomes more than historical detail, it becomes a prophetic mirror of a far greater reality. Mordecai's procession through the city foreshadows the humility and exaltation of Christ Himself.

Both moments mark turning points in redemptive history: one within Persia's walls, and the other upon Jerusalem's streets.

- Mordecai, the faithful servant once forgotten, is exalted in royal garments.

- Christ, the suffering Servant despised by men, enters the city clothed in humility.

Each prefigures victory through humility and triumph through surrender.

"Behold, your King is coming to you... humble and riding on a donkey." ~ Zechariah 9:9

Even the words spoken over Mordecai, *"the man whom the king delights to honor,"* reflect the voice of the Father over the Son: *"This is My beloved Son, in whom I am well pleased." ~Matthew 3:17*

Mordecai's quiet obedience mirrors the submission of Christ in which both are honored not for ambition, but for faithfulness.

Temporal Reward vs. Eternal Inheritance

Jesus' words in Matthew 6:1–4 expose the difference between worldly reward and spiritual inheritance: *"They have their reward."*

Haman's glory is fleeting, applause that fades before the ink of the decree barely has time to dry. His reward is hollow because it was rooted in self-exaltation. But Mordecai's honor, like righteousness itself, comes not from striving but from surrender. So, his name endures not because he demanded it, but because he trusted God's timing.

It is the same law of grace Paul captures in Philippians: *"He humbled Himself... therefore God highly exalted Him."* ~Philippians 2:8–9

So humility precedes glory, not as moral advice, but as spiritual law:

- Mordecai humbles himself at the gate, and is exalted before the city.
- Christ humbles Himself to death, and is exalted to the right hand of God.
- Haman exalts himself before men, and is humiliated before both God and man.
- This is the very rhythm of spiritual justice in which reversal is born through humility.

The Collapse of Pride

When the king commands Haman to do all these things for Mordecai, the narrative reaches its emotional breaking point. You can almost feel the air leave the room. For Haman—the man whose pride has filled every scene—this command is not merely humiliating; it is annihilating.

His entire identity was built upon control, power, and perception. And now, in a single sentence, it all collapses.

"Pride goes before destruction, and a haughty spirit before a fall." ~ Proverbs 16:18

Just hours earlier, Haman was plotting Mordecai's death and rushing the construction of the gallows. Yet before the night is through, his plans are overturned, and the man he sought to destroy rides in royal splendor through the city. So, what he built for another becomes his own undoing.

The Faith of Mordecai

Meanwhile, Mordecai is likely stunned. The summons he receives must have seemed ominous, and though his faith was steady, his human heart remained uncertain. Faith, after all, does not always calm the nerves; it steadies the will.

Hebrews 11 reminds us that faith is not the absence of fear, but endurance beneath it. Mordecai's obedience positions him for reward, even when he expects condemnation.

This moment becomes a living parable of Romans 8:1: *"There is therefore now no condemnation for those who are in Christ Jesus."*

What he thought would be his downfall becomes his deliverance, and what he expected as judgment becomes glory. This is the paradox of grace:

- What we fear most—judgment—becomes the pathway to life.
- What we think will condemn us becomes the place where God reveals His glory.

"For God did not send His Son into the world to condemn the world, but to save the world through Him." ~ John 3:17

"Those He justified, He also glorified." ~ Romans 8:30

134

Such is the nature of grace, it overturns the sentence of death and rewrites it as deliverance.

The Parade of Honor

At last, the two men come face to face, likely for the first time since their enmity began. Haman, the architect of destruction, must now lead the one he hates through the streets in celebration.

The irony is inescapable. The accuser becomes the announcer, and the proud becomes the herald of the humble. The same voice that demanded Mordecai's death now pro-claims his honor before all of Susa. And this is the gospel pattern in what the enemy means for humiliation, God turns into enthronement.

Haman, the archetype of Satan, becomes the unwilling herald of God's chosen servant. As he parades Mordecai through the city, he unknowingly re-enacts a cosmic truth, and one that will culminate centuries later when every power of darkness bows before the risen Christ.

"At the name of Jesus every knee should bow, in heaven and on earth and under the earth." ~Philippians 2:10

Even the unwilling will one day become witnesses to His glory. So, what was meant for shame becomes a stage for redemption. And once again, the story of Esther points for-ward not only to the rescue of a people, but to the triumph of a King.

The Signet, the Robes, and the Mount

As Mordecai is clothed, crowned, and paraded through the city, the author's details are more than ceremonial, they are theological. Each element—the robe, the horse, the crown, and the proclamation—reveals layers of meaning that reverberate far beyond the Persian court.

1. The Robes — Clothed in Righteousness

In Persian custom, wearing the king's robe was no small gesture.

It symbolized the transfer of royal favor and authority, marking the wearer as one who stood in the king's stead. So, Mordecai, once over-looked and forgotten, now becomes the visible bearer of the king's righteousness. This moment is deeply typological in that it mirrors the believer's own spiritual reality.

"He has clothed me with the garments of salvation; He has covered me with the robe of righteousness." ~ Isaiah 61:10

Just as Mordecai is covered in royal garments not his own, we too are clothed in the righteousness of Christ through an unearned exchange of God's favor. His covering becomes our confidence.

2. The Horse — Power in Motion

The royal horse symbolized strength, dominion, and move-ment—a declaration that the one who rides is commissioned by the throne. Yet, where Mordecai rides in imperial splendor, Christ enters Jerusalem on a donkey.

This contrast is intentional. Mordecai's exaltation dis-plays power granted, and Christ's procession reveals power restrained.

One rides in the authority of an earthly king while the other in the meekness of Heaven's King.

The inversion is beautiful:

- Mordecai's moment foreshadows Christ's, yet the true King comes not in conquest, but in peace.
- Both rides mark legitimacy of kingship, yet one empire fades while the other is eternal.

3. The Crown (Signet) — Suffering Before Glory

Some translations call it a "royal crest" or "diadem." Whether crown or emblem, the symbol represents delegated sovereignty, and Mordecai wears what once belonged to the king. But the gospel pattern takes this image even further: Christ, before being crowned in glory, is crowned with thorns. His suffering precedes exaltation. So, the mocking crown becomes the doorway to the true one. And the righteous sufferer, whether Mordecai or Christ, bears the pattern of spiritual reversal via humiliation giving way to glory.

4. The Proclamation — The Delight of the King

As the herald cries, *"Thus shall it be done to the man whom the king delights to honor,"* the language itself feels prophetic. It echoes another voice from Heaven: *"This is My beloved Son, in whom I am well pleased." ~Matthew 3:17*

Both scenes carry the same heartbeat in which royal delight precedes public exaltation. In both, the one being honored has already proven faithful.

- The human king delights to honor his loyal servant.
- The eternal King delights to glorify His obedient Son.

This is the spiritual order of grace: obedience followed by delight, humility followed by honor.

The Deeper Parallel — Glory Born Out of Humiliation

Both Mordecai's procession and Christ's triumphal entry are moments of paradox where exaltation emerges from the soil of suffering. Each scene foreshadows the mystery of glory born from humility.

- Mordecai's honor precedes Haman's downfall.
- Christ's entry precedes His crucifixion—and through it, Satan's defeat.

In both, God uses public spectacle to reveal spiritual victory. Mordecai's ride through Susa becomes a prophetic reflection of Calvary's triumph, where the true King will be *"lifted up" (John 12:32)*, not upon a royal mount, but upon a cross.

The pattern repeats throughout Scripture:

- Joseph rises from the pit to the palace.
- Daniel goes from the lion's den to royal favor.
- Mordecai moves from the gate to the king's horse.
- Christ ascends from the tomb to the throne.

This is the rhythm of redemption: exaltation through descent, victory through surrender, and life through death. And this is the very picture of baptism itself.

138

The Mourning of Haman

After the procession, Haman returns home in despair. The text says, *"He covered his head and mourned."* This single phrase reveals more than emotion, it marks the death of pride. If he were merely humiliated, he might have raged or plotted revenge.

But mourning implies something deeper: grief unto death. His covering of the head signifies resignation, and the acknowledgment that his downfall has begun. This reversal runs parallel to Mordecai's earlier grief:

- Mordecai tore his garments in grief for his people.
- Haman covers his head in grief for himself.

One mourns out of love; the other out of loss. This contrast exposes the moral divide between godly sorrow and worldly sorrow.

"Godly sorrow produces repentance... but worldly sorrow produces death." ~2 Corinthians 7:10

Mordecai's mourning led to deliverance, while Haman's mourning leads to destruction. Therefore, the open heart receives redemption while the closed one seals its own judgment.

A Man Becomes the Omen

Yet, the irony further deepens. The man who once sought omens through divination now becomes one himself. Ha-man's earlier casting of lots (Pur) was an attempt to control fate, and to manipulate the heavens. But now, providence turns him into the embodiment of his own superstition. What he once sought in secret has manifested before his eyes. He is the omen of his own ruin.

"Let now the astrologers, the stargazers stand up and save you... you are wearied with your many counsels." ~ Isaiah 47:12–13

The one who trusted in omens now drowns in them. And his "many counsels" have exhausted him, leaving him trapped under inevitability. Superstition and pride share the same root in which both try to control what only God governs. Now, in poetic justice, the manipulator becomes the message.

Zeresh's Prophetic Counsel

When Haman's wife and friends hear what has happened, their tone shifts entirely. The same voices that once fueled his pride now pronounce his downfall: *"If Mordecai, before whom you have begun to fall, is of the seed of the Jews, you will not prevail against him but will surely fall before him."* ~Esther 6:13

It is the first time they speak truth, but only because judgment is already inevitable. Their words become prophetic without them realizing it. Even pagan lips can declare the victory of covenant promise. And the counsel that once fed his ambition now confirms his doom. And this moment captures the complete disintegration of pride's illusion.

"Blessed is the man who does not walk in the counsel of the wicked."
~Psalm 1:1

Counsel as a Spiritual Motif in Esther

From the very beginning, counsel has been one of the book's defining threads. Every major turning point, and every rise and fall begins with conversation. The voices surrounding each character shape their destiny.

- Ahasuerus (Xerxes) Listens to flattering advisors (1:13–21)
- Esther Listens to Mordecai and the Eunuch (2:10; 4:14–16)
- Haman Listens to Zeresh and his friends (5:14; 6:13)

Each person's advisors mirror the posture of their heart. As Proverbs 13:20 teaches, *"He who walks with the wise grows wise, but a companion of fools suffers harm."*

The theme of counsel becomes a mirror for the reader as well: whose voices shape your decisions? Because in Esther, counsel is never neutral, it always leads either toward covenant faithfulness or toward destruction.

The "Wise Men" of Council

As the chapter nears its close, the irony deepens as Haman calls for his "wise men." But their wisdom is nothing more than polished foolishness. Their counsel, wrapped in flattery, lacks discernment entirely. And the author uses this title, *"wise men,"* deliberately and ironically. It's the same kind of mockery found in Paul's words: *"For the wisdom of this world is foolishness to God."* ~ *1 Corinthians 3:19*

These men mirror Pharaoh's magicians, who mimicked miracles but missed the message, and Job's friends, who spoke with intellect but without revelation. They have knowledge, but no insight. And their counsel sounds wise but leads to ruin. Haman surrounds himself with people who affirm his illusion of greatness, not those who would ever challenge it.

So, their "counsel" is not conversation, it's an echo chamber. And in that silence, the text reveals a sobering truth in which pride does not seek wisdom, it seeks validation. And when vali-dation becomes counsel, destruction follows.

This stands in sharp contrast to Esther. Her counselors — Mordecai and her attendants — speak few words, but each carries weight. She listens, she ponders, and she acts with discernment. Her silence, too, becomes its own kind of wisdom through the stillness of humility against the noise of pride. So, where Haman's circle feeds ego, Esther's circle cultivates obedience. Both are surr-ounded by voices, but only one hears the truth.

Zeresh's Two Speeches

Furthermore, Zeresh — the very voice that fueled Haman's arrogance — becomes the unwitting herald of his doom. Her tone changes from flattery to fatalism, completing the reversal that runs throughout the chapter:

- The king who forgets remembers.
- The righteous man who mourns is exalted.
- The proud man who boasts mourns his own death.
- The wife who once encouraged ambition now prophesies its consequence.

Everything that once empowered Haman now turns against him. His wealth, his influence, and even his relation-ships all crumble beneath the weight of reversal. So Zeresh's voice thus bookends Haman's story like a hinge on which his fortune swings.

- In Chapter 5, her counsel builds his pride: *"Have a gallows made!"*
- In Chapter 6, her counsel breaks his spirit: *"You will surely fall before him."*

This repetition isn't coincidence, it's narrative design. Each speech marks a turning of timing: the first fuels his haste while the second seals his fate. Zeresh's sudden shift fulfills Proverbs 19:21: *"Many are the plans in a man's heart, but it is the Lord's purpose that prevails."* So, even the voices of the wicked, in the end, testify to the supremacy of God's will.

The Collapse of Worldly Counsel

In Chapter 5, Zeresh's advice made sense. It was strategic, pragmatic, and self-serving. But worldly wisdom cannot survive God's sovereignty. So, what was once shrewd collapses under the weight of providence.

"There is no wisdom, no understanding, and no counsel against the Lord." ~Proverbs 21:30

All counsel detached from righteousness leads to ruin, no matter how clever it sounds. When sin is judged, every partnership built on pride disintegrates. Flattery flees when favor fades.

In Esther 6:13, even the language shifts. Zeresh and the "wise men" no longer speak *to* Haman but *about* him; a linguistic distancing that mirrors the moral one. Notice how her tone moves from co-conspirator to bystander, and from intimate counsel to detached prophecy.

Where she once said, *"Let a gallows be made,"* she now says, *"If Mordecai is of the Jews..."* She no longer identifies with his ambition, only with the inevitability of his downfall.

It echoes Revelation 18:9–10, where the kings of the earth who once shared Babylon's luxuries now stand afar as they watch its destruction, saying, *"Woe, woe!"*

Zeresh becomes a prophet of "Babylon's" fall, forced to declare truth she does not comprehend. So, God allows evil to craft the instruments of its own undoing. Every plan Haman devised — every word of counsel, every flattery, even the gallows — now turns against him.

"He who digs a pit will fall into it; his mischief will return upon his own head." ~ Psalm 7:15–16

And the banquet that once inflated his pride now calls him to judgment. The same invitation that marked his triumph now drags him toward his end. And the symbol of worldly pleasure — the feast — becomes the courtroom of Haman's own judgement.

Closing Remarks

The villains of the story often feel distant from us as readers, and understandably so. They tend to exist in our minds as moral extremes—dark figures so far removed from reason that we can hardly relate to them. They hiss at the mention of good or light, and in contrast, we instinctively see ourselves among the heroes or heroines instead.

Yet what makes a villain truly compelling is not their placement as the antagonist, but what they reveal about the complexity of the human condition. Rarely do we identify with the villains. We try to find ourselves in the courage of Esther, the faith of Abraham, or the devotion of David—but never in the Pharaohs, the Hamans, or the Judases of Scripture.

But the truth is, we are far more like them than we think. And perhaps it's precisely because we are so much like them that we should pay closer attention to what their stories are showing us.

While the villains certainly carry archetypal weight, their humanity often reveals a moral far deeper than the heroes themselves. Apart from the intervention of God, there is little that separates the "hero" from the "villain." In many cases, the heroes of Scripture were just as flawed, and sometimes worse, than the enemies they opposed.

Abraham was rebuked by a pagan king for lying. Saul sought counsel from a witch when he could no longer hear from God. David took Bathsheba for himself and sent her husband to die.

And yet, time and time again, these same men are remembered for their faith while their enemies are crushed beneath the weight of God's justice.

So what sets them apart from their enemies?

It is God Himself.

It has always been God who extends the invitation and intervenes on their behalf. It often takes the span of their entire lives to even begin to grasp His goodness in the midst of their failures. Each one is plucked from the fire and reshaped by His hand through the long work of sanctification.

And notice how God never erases their human nature. He works through it. Every so often, the habits of the old self rise again, but God redeems even those moments for His glory. And over time, their hearts grow softer and more yielded to His purpose.

That's why the stories of the villains are so sobering. Because through them, we glimpse what becomes of the heart left unyielded. They are not merely sources of conflict to the heroes, they are reflections of what we could become if left to ourselves.

This is what made Jesus' words to the Pharisees so un-bearable to them. When He called them "whitewashed tombs" and likened their hearts to Pharaoh's, He forced them to see themselves in the reflection of those they despised. Never could they have imagined that the very condition which once enslaved their ancestors was alive within them.

And that is the sobering reality still, that apart from Christ, we are each just as capable of becoming more like Haman than like Esther or Mordecai.

REFLECTION & DISCUSSION

1. Mordecai's remembrance reminds us that heaven records righteousness long before earth rewards it.

   What acts of quiet faithfulness in your life might God be writing into His book of remembrance, even if no one else ever acknowledges them?

2. Haman's downfall began not with failure, but with counsel that echoed his pride.

   Whose voices most shape your decisions today, and do they challenge your heart toward humility or confirm your desire for control?

3. The robe, the horse, and the crown all symbolize what only God can bestow: true honor that flows from obedience, not ambition.

   Where in your life have you sought to wear a "robe" of recognition that God has not yet placed upon you, and how can you return that desire to Him?

4. Zeresh's final words remind us that even worldly wisdom must one day bow to God's sovereignty.

When the plans you've built begin to collapse under God's redirection, will you resist in pride like Haman, or yield in trust like Mordecai, believing that His remembrance is greater than your reputation?

5. The villains of Scripture reveal what becomes of the heart left unyielded to God.

    When you read the story of Haman, or any who fell through pride, do you see only their downfall, or do you allow their reflection to expose what still needs surrender within your own heart?

CHAPTER SEVEN

The Bride and the Accuser

So the king and Haman entered to feast and drink with Queen Esther. ~Esther 7:1

The Banquet

The next chapter opens on the heels of one of the most ironic reversals in Scripture. Haman, who had spent the previous day consumed by rage and humiliation, now finds himself summoned im-mediately to the feast Esther had prepared. His face is likely still pale from mourning his own pride, yet he must compose himself, put on his courtly smile, and pretend that all is well. He reminds himself that this banquet is, after all, in his honor—or so he believes. The weight of despair clings to him, but he covers it with the mask of dignity, hoping that ceremony might dull the sting of exposure.

Esther, meanwhile, stands in quiet tension of her own. The previous chapter ended with victory in heaven's eyes, but her trial on earth is not yet complete. She has fasted, prayed, and found favor with the king once before, yet now she must step into the moment that will determine the fate of her people. Though God's providence is clearly at work behind the scenes, her humanity still trembles under the weight of what must be said. Like Haman, she too wears a mask—but hers is not deceit. It is composure under pressure, the calm of obedience wrapped around a heart that still fears.

Both Haman and Esther are entering the same room, facing the same king, yet their motives are worlds apart. Haman hides corruption while Esther hides courage. He masks decay and she masks devotion. The banquet thus becomes the setting of exposure, where the outer layer of every heart is stripped away.

The symmetry is deliberate. What unfolds in Esther 7 is not simply the downfall of a man or the vindication of a woman, it is the revelation of what has been hidden all along. The spiritual battlefield first manifests within the human heart before it ever reaches the realm of circumstance. Ha-man's war has never been just against Mordecai; it is against humility itself. His pride must be unmasked, and his false glory undone. And Esther's courage, buried under fear and restraint, must be revealed for what it truly is; a vessel for God's deliverance.

This internal contrast—despair veiled as confidence, and faith veiled as silence—reveals one of Scripture's oldest patterns. Before truth is revealed, both good and evil wear disguises. Adam and Eve hid in the garden, cloaking guilt with fig leaves. Saul hid behind zeal, mistaking passion for righteousness. Even the disciples, before Pentecost, hid be-hind locked doors, unaware that resurrection power already waited on the other side of fear.

So it is here in Susa. A queen and a courtier both sit before the throne where one is about to intercede for life while the other is condemned by his own deception. This moment, heavy with irony and tension, reminds us that before every revelation of God's justice, there comes an unveiling of the heart. The scene, therefore, does not begin with action, but with posture.

Standing Before the Throne

The scene then unfolds like a courtroom—quiet and tense. Esther stands before two powers: the king who holds her fate and the accuser who seeks her destruction. Yet even before she opens her mouth, her case has already been won. The moment the king raised his scepter back in chapter five, grace was already granted. The verdict of favor had already been spoken. So, what she now steps into is not a plea for acceptance, but the *expression* of it. Her intercession is not the earning of mercy, but the outworking of mercy already received.

This subtle distinction transforms the entire landscape. Esther is not standing as a beggar at the throne but as one who already bears the seal of royal approval. Her fear may still run through her body, but in the eyes of the king, she stands justified. The outcome is settled before the argument begins. This is the paradox of faith— where grace precedes defense, and victory precedes the battle.

It is courtroom imagery that reaches far beyond Persia's palace. In Esther, we glimpse a pattern that mirrors the spiritual order of redemption. Humanity, too, stands between a King and an accuser—between the righteous Judge and the one who hurls condemnation. And just like Esther, we find that our standing does not rest on persuasion or performance, but on favor already extended.

When Jesus declared, *"And I, when I am lifted up from the earth, will draw all men unto Me" (John 12:32),* He was speaking of that same exchange. The lifting was both crucifixion and coronation through an image of suffering enthroned. It was at the cross that justice met mercy, that wrath bowed before love, and that the King extended His scepter toward all who would come. What looked like defeat was, in truth, the declaration of victory.

Revelation gives us the other half of that same pattern. There, the accuser is *cast down*—the one who once stood before the throne to condemn the saints now silenced forever. Once Christ ascended and took His seat, the courtroom of heaven changed forever. The gavel fell not in judgment against us, but in the final dismissal of our accuser's claims.

"They overcame him by the blood of the Lamb and by the word of their testimony." ~Revelation 12:11

Both scenes in which Christ is lifted up and Satan is cast down, speak the same truth that the trial is already over. The verdict has been sealed by favor. Esther's raised scepter in chapter five becomes the Old Testament shadow of the cross itself, and the moment grace was extended long before the plea was spoken.

And so, when Esther stands before both king and accuser, the true battle has already been won. Her act of courage flows not *toward* grace but *from* it. She stands in the tension of appearance and reality in which she is appearing vulnerable yet she spiritually vindicated.

This is the lesson that humbles every believer: accusation only has power where remembrance fades. The enemy's voice grows loud only when we forget the decree already written over us which is that we are chosen, covered, and called righteous by the One who reigns.

The king's words in verse two confirm this: his favor still stands and his invitation is still open. Just as before, he offers her everything— *"even to half the kingdom."* His patience mirrors God's own, steady and un-changing. Esther's voice may tremble, but his mercy does not.

In that moment, she—and we—are reminded that our hesitation never diminishes His invitation. The throne of grace does not waver when we do. The scepter remains extended. The verdict remains sealed. And grace, once given, never withdraws its reach.

The Intercession of the Bride

When Esther finally speaks in verses 3 and 4, her words cut through the air with measured precision. The mask of composure falls away, and what stands revealed is not a plea born of fear, but a declaration shaped by conviction. She reveals the decree of death hanging over her people and, with stunning restraint, makes a chilling observation: *"For we are sold, I and my people, to be destroyed, to be slain, and to perish. But if we had been sold merely as slaves, I would have held my peace."*

That small distinction is profound. Slavery, though cruel, would not have warranted interrupting the king's peace—but death itself demanded confrontation. What's at stake is not mere oppression but obliteration. Esther discerns something deeper than politics; she sees the true aim of the enemy. The plot is not just to subjugate but to erase, and to silence the covenant people entirely.

This moment exposes the spiritual logic behind all of evil's schemes. From Pharaoh's order to drown the Hebrew sons, to Herod's massacre of infants, to the serpent's deceit in Eden—the pattern is the same. The adversary does not settle for enslavement; his goal is annihilation. The aim of darkness has always been the destruction of God's image-bearers and the nullifying of His covenant promises.

In standing before the throne, Esther becomes far more than a desperate queen, she becomes a type of Christ. She does not argue for her own innocence or her people's merit; she pleads on the basis of identity and covenant. Her words mirror the intercession of the greater Mediator to come.

"He ever lives to make intercession for them."
~Hebrews 7:25

Like Esther, Jesus stands between judgment and mercy, between a righteous King and a condemned people. But un-like Esther, He does not plead for deliverance from another's decree, He fulfills the decree Himself. He takes upon His own body the sentence written against us. So, what Esther does in shadow, Christ completes in substance.

Her courage, then, is not just an act of rescue but of representation. She becomes the vessel through which mercy meets accusation. Her willingness to stand in the gap for her people reveals the heartbeat of intercession—the moment when love stands between wrath and ruin.

And listen again to her words: *"We are sold... to be destroyed, to be slain, and to perish."* They speak across time as a portrait of the human condition before redemption. We, too, were enslaved under the decree of death, sold under sin, and destined for destruction. But then came the greater Esther.

"The thief comes only to steal, kill, and destroy; I have come that they may have life, and have it abundantly." ~John 10:10

In this light, Esther's intercession becomes more than a moment of courage, it becomes prophecy. She foreshadows the day when another would stand before the throne, not clothed in royal robes but in flesh, and silence the accuser forever. Her plea interrupts the plot of destruction, just as Christ's cross interrupted the curse of death.

There is, therefore, now no condemnation for those who are in Him ~Romans 8:1

For the decree of death has already been overturned by the decree of grace. And the King, having extended His scepter once for all, will not withdraw it again.

The King's Response — Relationship Over Heritage

When the king rises in fury and demands, *"Who is he, and where is he who would dare presume in his heart to do so?" (Esther 7:5),* there's a detail easy to overlook. Notice how he never asks *who* Esther is. He doesn't inquire about her nationality, her lineage, or her right to stand before him. None of that matters. What matters is *who dares threaten her.*

Throughout the book of Esther, identity has been a dividing line: Jew versus Gentile, servant versus noble, and insider versus outcast. Mordecai's faith made him despised, Haman's heritage as an Agagite became his weapon of pride, and Esther's concealed background stood as both her protection and her risk. Yet in this moment, the king strips all of that away. He does not see labels or lineage. He sees his bride.

It's as though his heart shouts through the text: *"I don't care where you come from. I only care who dares threaten what is mine."*

This is covenant language, not possessive in the worldly sense, but protective in the spiritual one. His question reveals the essence of faithful love and the impulse to defend, to cover, and to preserve what has been joined to oneself. It's the same tone heard in the voice of God throughout Scripture when He calls Israel *"My people"* or the Church *"My bride."* In both cases, the relationship overrides every other identity marker.

Christ and His Bride

This scene mirrors the believer's standing before Christ. When the accuser stands before the throne to condemn us, the King of Glory does not examine our past, our origin, or our failures. He does not say, "Where are you from?" He says, "Who dares accuse My beloved?"

Our identity, therefore, is not measured by where we've come from, but by *Whose* we've become. In Christ, the question of belonging has already been answered, the scepter has already been extended, and the robe has already been placed on our shoulders. To the King, Esther's worth was not up for debate, and neither is ours.

"That He might present the church to Himself in splendor, without spot or wrinkle or any such thing, but that she might be holy and without blemish." ~ Ephesians 5:27

The Battle for Identity

This exchange also reveals one of the enemy's oldest strategies. From Eden to the wilderness, his first weapon has always been identity distortion.

"Did God really say?"

"If You are the Son of God..."

The devil doesn't need to strip power if he can make us doubt identity, because every victory of faith flows from knowing who you are and Whose you are.

That's why this moment in Esther is more than royal drama, it's spiritual warfare. So the king's question, *"Who is he that dares presume?"* is Heaven's rebuke to every voice that tries to redefine God's chosen.

"Who shall bring a charge against God's elect? It is God who justifies. Who is he that condemns?" ~Romans 8:33–34

In the heavenly courtroom, the accuser's case collapses under the weight of that question.

Grace Replaces Lineage

And the beauty of this passage is that Esther's Jewish identity—once her greatest liability—becomes the vessel of deliverance. The very thing she was told to conceal becomes the key to redemption. Her hiddenness was not denial; it was protection until the appointed time.

And So it is with us. Our identity was hidden with Christ until the day of revelation (Colossians 3:3). When grace called our name, and what once marked us for judgment now marks us for inheritance.

If our life is in Christ, then no power—earthly or spiritual—can stand against us. We have died with Him, been raised with Him, and now live in Him (Romans 6:5–8; Galatians 2:20). Our identity is no longer fragile or conditional; it is resurrected.

That is the power of covenant love.

It reframes prayer not as pleading for acceptance, but as standing in acceptance already given. It transforms uncertain-ty into confidence, not because we are strong, but because the One who holds the scepter calls us His own. So, the King's question still reverberates through time: *"Who dares threaten what is Mine?"*

The Fulfillment of Fear and the Unraveling of Pride

Haman's downfall in verse 6 is not abrupt, it's the slow and inevitable culmination of what's been festering within him since chapter 5. The seed of pride has finally borne its bitter fruit. What he feared most—that he might be shamed, exposed, and stripped of control—has now come to pass. His fear has become prophecy. And the very thing he dreaded has become the means of his undoing.

"A man's pride shall bring him low, but honor shall uphold the humble in spirit." ~Proverbs 29:23

Pride always constructs its own gallows. Haman's humiliation is not a random reversal; it's spiritual symmetry. He exalted himself through manipulation, but in doing so, constructed the very platform that would become his scaffold.

The Loss of Access

Once, Haman enjoyed full and uninhibited access to the king. His proximity symbolized privilege, but privilege is not the same as covenant.

159

Haman's position was political while Esther's was relational. He was close through human favor, but she was near through God's grace.

Haman's access came from merit and Esther's came from mercy.

When the moment of reckoning arrives, Haman finds himself speechless before the king. He has no defense, no appeal, and no claim to intimacy. His title cannot save him. His influence cannot speak for him. This is what happens when access is built on self instead of covenant in which proximity without relationship eventually collapses.

In contrast, Esther stands with quiet confidence, not because she is flawless, but because she is favored. The king has already extended his kingdom to her. His scepter of grace reached her long before this moment, and that grace remains unshaken in the face of accusation.

This mirrors the spiritual reality of the believer's standing before God.

"The accuser of our brothers has been cast down, who accused them day and night before our God. And they overcame him by the blood of the Lamb and the word of their testimony."
~Revelation 12:10

The enemy's voice was silenced, not through debate, but through covenant. His right to accuse ended the moment grace entered the court-room.

"Through Him we have obtained access by faith into this grace in which we stand." ~Romans 5:2

That single word—*access*—divides the two worlds of Esther and Haman. Haman's access was revoked because it was built on pride. Esther's was secured because it was received through surrender.

The Bride and the Accuser

The scene is filled with contrast and revelation. Haman stands as the embodiment of accusation, self-exaltation, and human striving. Esther stands as the image of intercession, humility, and spiritual favor.

When she speaks, accusation collapses. When she stands, condemnation loses its voice. This is the heartbeat of New Test-ament theology hidden in Old Testament imagery.

The Bride's authority does not come from argument or worth—it comes from covenantal intimacy with the King. Her standing silences accusation, not because evil ceases to speak, but because its words no longer have ground to stand on.

This moment in Esther is a shadow of the Church's triumph in Christ. The closer the Bride stands to the throne, the weaker the enemy's voice becomes. Therefore, intimacy with the King neutralizes accusation because grace renders guilt powerless.

Proximity alone is not enough—Haman had that. Only intimacy secures belonging—Esther had that. And that difference defines the entire outcome of their lives. One sought recognition while the other rested in relationship. One trusted ambition, and the other trusted in grace.

What unfolds here is not just a political reversal, it's a covenant revelation: those who build their worth on pride are destined to fall, but those who anchor their identity in grace will always rise.

The Eruption of Chaos

Verses 7–8 then erupt like thunder after a long, tightening silence. The tension that has been mounting since chapter 5 finally reaches its breaking point. And everything Haman has sown—his pride, deceit, fear, and self-exaltation—detonates in one desperate, chaotic moment. What began as a banquet of celebration becomes the stage of his unraveling.

And it's important to note that the King's wrath is not random here; it's cumulative. Xerxes has endured defeat after defeat through humiliation in his Greek campaign, unrest within his empire, conspiracies in his palace, and now betrayal at his own table. For a man who thrives on control, this moment strikes the deepest wound possible. The treachery has reached his most sacred space: his feast, his authority, and his bride. The text captures a breaking point not just of anger, but of identity.

The king who rules nations cannot rule his own house.

And so, his wrath explodes not just as a political response, but as a human reaction to profound betrayal. His pride and pain converge in fury, but even here, the scene pulls our eyes higher to a greater parallel through God's own jealousy.

Wrath Born from Betrayal

Xerxes' rage may seem impulsive, but underneath it beats some-thing universally human which is the ache of betrayal and the instinct to defend what one loves. In his flawed, earthly way, he mirrors a higher truth of the covenant jealousy of God. Scripture repeatedly portrays God's wrath not as arbitrary anger but as the zeal of a husband defending His bride.

> *"For the LORD your God is a consuming fire, a jealous God."*
> *~Deuteronomy 4:24*

> *"For Zion's sake I will not keep silent, and for Jerusalem's sake*
> *I will not rest." ~Isaiah 62:1*

This moment in Esther becomes a vivid metaphor for that holy fire. Haman's treachery violates not just royal order but covenant imagery. The feast—the symbol of comm-union—is desecrated. The bride—the image of covenant love—is endangered. And the King, whose patience has reached its limit, rises in jealous defense.

It's a terrifying yet sobering image of God's love. The wrath of God is not the absence of love but its fiercest expression through a kind of love that will not permit corruption to touch what it calls its own.

The Accuser Clinging to the Bride

Then comes one of the most ironic and haunting moments in all of Esther. Haman, now fully exposed, throws himself upon

Esther in desperation. What looks like a plea for mercy becomes an act of defilement. The irony is painful because the very man who sought to destroy the covenant people now grasps at the embodiment of covenant favor.

On the surface, it's panic. But spiritually, it's prophetic. This is the image of the accuser grasping for what he can no longer possess. It's the desperate clinging of evil to the Bride of Christ through a futile attempt to corrupt what grace has already claimed.

Esther, likely frozen in fear and shock, cannot resist him. Yet even in that powerless posture, she is not unprotected. Her defense has already been secured by favor. This is the essence of spiritual security. Evil may press close; chaos may seem to overpower; yet the Bride remains untouched beneath the covering of the King's authority.

"He who touches you touches the apple of His eye."
~ Zechariah 2:8

"No weapon formed against you shall prosper."
~Isaiah 54:17

What Haman meant as a desperate grasp becomes his own death sentence. The moment he lays hold of the queen, his judgment is sealed.

The False Appearance of Violation

When the king returns and sees Haman thrown upon Esther, the text slows, almost cinematic in its intensity. He walks into a scene of chaos in which his bride pinned beneath the hand of the man who betrayed her. The sight alone is enough to enrage him beyond reason. Though it's important to note that no actual harm has been done. Yet appearance alone is enough.

This distinction is vital, because the scene operates on two levels—natural and spiritual. In the natural, the king sees apparent violation.

In the spiritual, it represents the enemy's attempt to desecrate the purity and identity of God's people. Sin, deception, and oppression often *appear* victorious. The Church, like Esther, may seem powerless or endangered. But the King's return—the moment of divine intervention—exposes illusion for what it is.

"For true and righteous are His judgments... for He has avenged the blood of His servants at her hand." ~Revelation 19:2

The same covenant justice beating in Revelation resounds here in Esther. The King's holy fury rises not in insecurity, but in defense of covenant love.

The Holy Fury of God's Protection

In human form, Xerxes' wrath is flawed and impulsive. But the spiritual reality it mirrors is perfect and unstoppable. God's wrath is not random, it is the righteous fire of love that refuses to let His bride be touched, defiled, or destroyed.

So, what unfolds here is the clearest image yet of that truth in which the King will not tolerate violation of His covenant. Every force that attempts to lay hands upon the Bride of Christ will face His consuming justice.

What terrifies Haman stands as comfort for the redeem-ed. Because the same wrath that consumes the accuser secures the beloved.

This is the great reversal of Esther 7: The accuser grasps the Bride, and the King rises. The enemy touches covenant, and judgment is triggered. And the wrath of God's love meets the desperation of evil, and the story shifts forever.

The Erasure of a Name

When the text says that Haman's face is covered and he is restrained, it marks more than a moment of political downfall, it signals theological erasure. In Scripture, to *blot out* a name was not merely to end a life, but to erase remembrance, lineage, and legacy. It was the severing of a name from covenant history and the removal of identity from under heaven.

This phrase appears repeatedly as the ultimate form of judgment:

- *"I will utterly blot out the remembrance of Amalek from under heaven." ~ Exodus 17:14*
- *"The LORD will blot out his name from under heaven." ~Deuteronomy 29:20*
- *"May they be blotted out of the book of life and not be listed with the righteous." ~Psalm 69:28*

So when Haman — the Agagite, the descendant of Amalek — is restrained and covered, the text is not simply closing his story; it is closing a bloodline.

The Amalekite defiance that began in Exodus now ends in Esther.

The covering of Haman's face is not only a gesture of humiliation, it is a prophetic act of obliteration. The face of the enemy, the voice of accusation, and the name that carried rebellion are removed from before the King.

The Covering of the Face

In ancient Near Eastern courts, the act of covering a condemned man's face carried heavy symbolism. It meant that he was no longer worthy to look upon the king. To be veiled was to be cut off, and to have one's light extinguished in the presence of glory.

The moment Haman's face is covered, his separation becomes complete. Once he moved freely in the royal court, cultivating schemes and manipulating power. Now, his sight is taken, his presence is concealed, and his voice is silenced. So, what grace had once allowed, judgment now forbids.

This is the spiritual counterpart to 2 Corinthians 3:18, where believers behold the glory of God with *unveiled faces*. In Christ, the veil is removed; in judgment, it is restored. Where grace gives access, sin enforces distance.

Haman — the archetype of the accuser — now wears the veil of separation. He mirrors the fate of Satan himself, cast from the courts of heaven, cut off from light, and barred from access to the throne. So, his covering marks not just death, but exile.

The Fulfillment of Covenant Vengeance

This moment also brings to completion one of the oldest promises in Scripture. In *Exodus 17:16,* God swore perpetual war against Amalek, the nation that ambushed Israel in the wilderness and sought to annihilate them. From that moment forward, Amalek became a living symbol of enmity against God's covenant people.

Haman, as *the Agagite,* carries that lineage, both physically and spiritually. So, his death is not random; it's covenantal. The war God declared in Exodus finds its resolution here in Persia. When Haman's face is covered and his name blotted out, the prophecy is fulfilled.

This is not vengeance in the petty, human sense. It's covenant justice, the divine completion of what God began long ago. And the same God who remembered Mordecai's loyalty also remembers His promise to erase the enemy of His people. In one act, remembrance and erasure meet in which the righteous are remembered, and the accuser is forgotten.

The Silencing of Accusation

Haman's physical restraint mirrors the spiritual restraint of the enemy in Revelation 20:2, where Satan is bound and silenced. Both acts serve the same purpose: to remove the accuser's ability to operate against the righteous.

"The accuser of our brothers has been cast down, who accused them before our God day and night." ~Revelation 12:10

In Esther 7, we witness the Old Testament fore-shadowing of that reality. The enemy who once spoke with authority is now voiceless. The one who orchestrated death is now covered in silence. The one who demanded recognition is now unseen. In other words, before the throne, accusation collapses into silence.

From Visibility to Disappearance

In literary terms, this is poetic justice in motion. The man who lived for visibility, who demanded that all bow before him, who built his identity on recognition and applause, now fades into obscurity. His face, once lifted high in arrogance, is covered. His name, once feared, is forgotten. And his glory, once celebrated, is erased forever.

It's the ultimate irony: the man who made visibility his god meets judgment through invisibility. So, the hidden are lifted, and the proud are cast down. It is the moral rhythm that drives the entire book of Esther in which God dismantles human glory until only His remains visible.

And so, as the veil falls over Haman's face, the spiritual veil is lifted for the reader, and the covenant war that began with Amalek ends here, not with battle, but with erasure. The accuser's name is gone, but God's remembrance endures for-ever.

The Narrative Pattern of Eunuchs

Throughout the book of Esther, eunuchs appear at every critical juncture; rarely in the spotlight, yet always positioned at the seams where heaven meets history. They are the quiet inter-mediaries, standing between command and fulfillment, secrecy and revelation, power and purpose. Each one occupies a liminal space, bridging what is unseen with what will soon be made visible.

So, by the time we reach chapter 7, the naming of *Harbona* is no incidental detail. His presence signals that Haman's downfall is not coincidence, but providential orchestration. The eunuchs have functioned as invisible conduits of providence from the be-ginning, each one a mirror of spiritual office.

- Chapter 2: Hegai prepares Esther — *favor and sanctification.*
- Chapter 4: Hathach mediates between Mordecai and Esther — *intercession and obedience.*
- Chapter 6: Bigthana and Teresh plot death at the gate — *corruption and contrast.*
- Chapter 7: Harbona speaks truth before the King — *revelation and justice.*

The pattern ascends: from the gate (the place of death) to the queen's side (the place of intercession), and finally to the throne (the place of judgment). What began in the outer courts now culminates in the presence of ultimate authority. It is a movement from hiddenness to full disclosure.

Harbona's Proximity to the Throne

Harbona is introduced as one who *stands in the king's presence.* In Persian court culture, only a select few eunuchs had such unrestricted access; not as participants, but as silent witnesses to royal will. They were attendants of justice, guardians of the unseen moments between decree and execution.

Harbona thus represents the *witness of justice*. When he speaks, the story pivots: *"Behold, the gallows that Haman has made for Mordecai, who spoke good on the king's behalf, stands at Haman's house." ~Esther 7:9*

This is not mere information; it is revelation. Harbona unmasks hidden sin and simultaneously names righteousness. His statement ex-poses the darkness of Haman's secret plot while affirming the light of Mordecai's virtue.

That dual act — *convicting the wicked and commending the righteous* — is precisely the ministry Jesus attributes to the Holy Spirit:

"When He comes, He will convict the world concerning sin and righteousness and judgment." ~John 16:8–11

In one breath, Harbona performs all three:
- Concerning sin — he reveals the gallows Haman built.
- Concerning righteousness — he recalls Mordecai's loyalty.
- Concerning judgment — he identifies the very instrument of Haman's execution.

He stands as a shadow of the Spirit: the revealer, the advocate, and the executor of divine justice. Even his name, *Harbona* (possibly meaning "donor" or "compassionate one"), reflects the Spirit's role as *giver and comforter.*

The Progression of Revelation

The eunuchs across *Esther* trace a pattern of unveiling:

- Hegai *prepares* the hidden vessel.
- Hathach *transmits* the hidden message.
- Harbona *reveals* the hidden judgment.

Each one marks a stage in the progressive revelation of God's plan. By Harbona's time, the veil between heaven's justice and earthly events is fully lifted.

> *"Nothing is covered up that will not be revealed, or hidden that will not be known." ~Luke 12:2–3*

So, what Haman built in secret — his gallows, his hatred, his pride — is now declared before the King's court by a servant who stands nearest the throne. The same principle governs the spiritual realm: the Holy Spirit brings to light every hidden work of darkness and aligns creation with God's truth.

From Accusation to Advocacy

Harbona's words are also more than observation, they are alignment. He speaks the righteousness of Mordecai before the King, reversing the narrative tone that once favored Ha-man's voice. Where Haman had slandered Mordecai, the King's servant now vindicates him. This exchange transforms the atmosphere of the throne room in which the voice of accusation is replaced by the voice of intercession.

*"The Spirit Himself intercedes for us... because He makes
intercession for the saints according to the will of God."*
~Romans 8:26–27

Harbona speaks not from personal allegiance, but from
spiritual agreement. His testimony resonates with the King's justice. It's what happens when truth finds its voice through faithful
servants and the court of heaven announces its verdict through
human vessels.

The Eunuch as Prophetic Office

The eunuchs in *Esther*—culminating in Harbona—thus
embody the prophetic role as servants without inheritance who
carry revelation from the throne to the people. They live in
proximity to power yet claim none of it for themselves.

*"To the eunuchs who keep My Sabbaths... I will give within
My temple a name better than sons and daughters."*
~Isaiah 56:4–5

That's Harbona's legacy — proximity rewarded with eternal
remembrance. He gains no earthly title, but his one act of truth
secures his name in Scripture as a witness to righteousness. He
stands as the archetype of every unseen servant who carries the
weight of revelation, and those who do not speak for personal gain,
but for God's justice.

Harbona as the Voice of the Spirit

In one verse, the tone of *Esther* shifts from political drama to spiritual allegory. Harbona becomes the voice that seals the verdict. He does not persuade or plead; he simply speaks what is true.

- He exposes hidden sin — "Behold, the gallows."
- He affirms righteousness — "Mordecai, who spoke good."
- He declares judgment — "It stands at Haman's house."

That tri-fold revelation is the utterance of the Spirit within the royal court through the hidden witness who testifies of truth at the moment evil collapses beneath it. Through Harbona, the narrative briefly parts its veil, letting the reader glimpse the eternal court-room beyond Persia's throne. And the servant's single line becomes heaven's decree:

"This is the one who has done good before the King." And in that simple statement, God's justice breathes through human history.

The Reversal Completed

The final verse of Esther 7 lands like a thunderclap. Haman is impaled on the very gallows he built, his body is lifted in the same posture of humiliation he once reserved for another. But this isn't poetic coincidence; it is the outworking of a spiritual principle that runs through all of Scripture.

"His mischief shall return upon his own head, and his violent dealing shall come down upon his own crown." ~Psalm 7:16

What the enemy designs for destruction becomes his own undoing. Haman's gallows is more than a wooden structure of death; it is a prophetic emblem of God's moral architecture in which the law of reversal is built into creation. The gallows becomes both judgment and prophecy, where evil collapses under its own weight. This is the summit of Esther's theme of reversal:

- The proud are brought low.
- The forgotten are remembered.
- The accuser is condemned by his own accusation.

So, the man who sought to lift himself high is now lifted up, not in honor, but in shame.

Collective Image of the Bride

The narrative does not end with an individual's vindication, but with a communal revelation. Mordecai's exaltation is not separate from Esther's intercession; the two together embody the full picture of covenant faithfulness.

Esther intercedes — the hidden life of communion and prayer. Mordecai is exalted — the visible testimony of righteousness and endurance.

Together, they form a composite image of the Bride of Christ — both the inward life of intimacy (Esther) and the outward witness of faith (Mordecai). One appeals before the throne; the other walks out that victory before the world.

So when Haman falls, he falls not merely before a man, but before the living representation of a covenant people, and before the reflection of faithfulness itself. His defeat is not personal; it is spiritual, cosmic, and prophetic.

The Gospel Foreshadowed

What the accuser had set for the accused, now stands as the very means of destruction for himself. And this is the very essence of the gospel embedded into this story. It's the same paradox that unfolds at Calvary.

Satan believed the crucifixion would be Christ's end and the silencing of righteousness. Yet that very cross became the weapon of his defeat. Death swallowed Life and choked.

Haman's gallows, in that sense, becomes a shadow of the Cross:

- It is built as a symbol of shame.
- It becomes the instrument of victory.
- It marks the moment where death begins to die.

The very tool of accusation becomes the altar of redemption. The gallows becomes a monument of reversal, and an emblem of a kingdom where mercy triumphs over judgment and justice outwits evil.

What Haman meant for silence becomes proclamation in which his impalement becomes his confession, and an acknowledgment that the throne of God's justice cannot be usurped.

The Prophecy Fulfilled

Even Haman's wife and companions foreshadowed his fate. In the previous chapter, Zeresh and his "wise men" spoke the truth they could not yet comprehend: *"If Mordecai is of the seed of the Jews, you will not prevail against him, but shall surely fall before him."*

Those words now return as prophecy fulfilled. The same voices that once urged him to build the gallows now fall silent in dread as they watch the irony unfold. So, Haman's end is not random, it was sown from the beginning. Every act of pride contained the seed of his own downfall. His ambition birthed the structure that would hang him, and his own hands crafted his sentence.

It is the same pattern that defines Satan's rebellion: pride leading to descent. The desire to ascend above the throne becomes the very cause of being cast down.

The Covenant Victory

The text then concludes with a final phrase that glows with theological weight: *"Then the king's wrath was pacified." ~Esther 7:10*

The Hebrew word *shakath* ("to subside, to be still") evokes the image of a storm finally calming after judgment, and the tempest of wrath yields to peace. The war of accusation gives way to covenant rest. This image repeats through all of redemptive history:

- After the flood, the waters subside and a rainbow seals the covenant.
- After the Red Sea, the waves close and Israel stands in silence.
- After the Cross, the earth trembles and then rests.

So too here, the wrath of the King quiets not through appeasement, but through justice fulfilled. The accuser's voice has been silenced, and peace returns to the court. It is the stillness after victory and the silence that follows when the gavel of heaven falls.

The Fate of the Accuser

Haman's death is not just a historical conclusion but a theological foreshadowing of ultimate eschatological truth.

"And the devil who deceived them was thrown into the lake of fire... and will be tormented day and night forever and ever."
~Revelation 20:10

The same structure is mirrored in Esther:

- The accuser's plot is exposed.
- His authority is stripped.
- His end comes by the very device he designed.

This is covenant symmetry in which evil collapses under its own rebellion while righteousness stands radiant. So, what began as a political narrative, closes with the fate of all accusation under the rule of God's justice.

The Crescendo of God's Reversal

This final scene seals the chapter's spiritual arc in perfect harmony with the book's grand design. The entire narrative crescendos into this paradox:

- The enemy's schemes destroy himself.
- The Bride stands vindicated.
- Justice flows from the throne.
- The King's peace returns.

What begins as hidden tension ends in unveiled triumph. The gallows of Haman become the cross-shaped echo of eternity, and the place where pride is buried, accusation silenced, and covenant love reigns supreme.

It is more than the end of a story. It is a miniature of redemption history itself, the eternal war between accusation and grace, pride and humility, death and life, all settled beneath the scepter of a faithful King.

CLOSING REMARKS

I don't think it's any coincidence that the culmination of this chapter stands with such a profound reflection as what culminated at the cross of Calvary. Everything that has happened thus far in the story of Esther represents a very familiar arc that has repeated all throughout Scriptural history, and what a beautiful picture it is.

Nothing stands outside the sovereignty of God. And I find that to be both utterly amazing and humbling all at once, because that means there is nothing I can do to escape Him. Yet it also means that there is nothing I can do to escape His love.

He has redeemed His people for Himself, and in so doing, He stands as our foremost Champion. It's not that He simply invites us in and prepares a feast for us, but that He clothes us with His own garments and His own inheritance. His crown, His authority, and most importantly—His Name—are offered to us for our very identity.

So often we hesitate to cross that threshold of invitation because we feel limited and disqualified by the marring of sin that stains our clothes and scars our skin with shame. But what a gift it is to know that as often as we have tried and tried to remove the stains from our garments—only to see them darken further, or bandage the wounds that fester to the depths of our soul—He offers Himself to us.

He offers us His own righteousness, His own purity, and His own authority to blot out any notion that we are irredeemable. He never asks us to clean ourselves up first or to present ourselves in a way that hides the existence of our heritage and broken past. Instead, He asks us for the fullness of it all.

It is a terrifying notion to relinquish the very parts of ourselves that we hold so deeply—our innermost shame and our deepest comfort in complacent guilt. These are, in essence, the parts that make us who we are. So to surrender them is to surrender the deepest and most vulnerable places of our soul. Yet who better to surrender them to than the One who knows our soul better than we ever could?

There is then no standard by which we can measure ourselves apart from Christ Himself. We are left to lay at the feet of His mercy, and when we cannot bear to look up—when the weight of our unworthiness shackles our eyes to the ground—He does something most unorthodox and unexpected.

He lays Himself down.

He takes the weight of our shame and guilt upon Him-self.

He breaks the bonds of our condemnation and says:

"See? There is no more shame and no accusation set against you. I have taken your place and your bonds upon Myself. Will you give Me your name, your past, your brokenness, and your heart? In return, I give you My own Name, My own honor, and My own robes to replace the ones you wear."

This is the very picture of the woman who knelt at Jesus' feet and could do nothing else but wash them with her tears and precious oil, wiping them with her hair. There were no words to say, and not even her eyes dared look up into His, for she knew too well the weight of her shame.

Yet He honored her, just as He honored the tax collector who beat his chest and cried out, *"God, be merciful to me, a sinner."* In both, He did what no other would ever offer.

He bridged the void between man and God; between proximity and intimacy. He said, *"Greater love has no man than this, that a man lay down his life for his friends. You are my friends..."*

And not long after, He was lifted up as the ultimate offering for atonement and sacrifice. He gave Himself for the world, for those like the woman at His feet and the tax collector who cried—and for those like you and me.

Then, at last, He offered us more still.

To rest.

To rest in Him, and to rest in the assurance of His love. His Word is true, and thus our hope is found in nothing less than the power of His Name and His resurrection. Death indeed could not hold Him. And when we are crucified with Christ, we too are raised with Him into new life.

Everything we claim as weakness and flaw, He has re-deemed and perfected through His righteousness alone. And for the one whom He claims as His own, none can pluck them from His hand.

REFLECTION & DISCUSSION

1. Both Esther and Haman enter the feast wearing masks—one concealing fear, the other pride.

   In what ways do you find yourself "masking" before God or others, and how might vulnerability before the King lead to freedom rather than exposure?

2. Esther stood between the King and her enemy already justified by grace.

   How does remembering that your "scepter has already been extended" change the way you face accusation, guilt, or spiritual warfare today?

3. When the king spoke, Haman's accusations lost all power.

   Whose voice shapes your sense of worth: the one that condemns, or the one that call you beloved? How can you train your heart to recognize the tone of the king over the lies of the enemy?

4. The very instrument Haman built became his undoing.

   Can you recognize areas in your life where God has turned what the enemy meant for harm into redemption or growth? What does that teach you about His sovereignty in your story?

5. The chapter ends with the King's wrath subsiding, and stillness after judgment.

    What does that stillness look like in your own life? Are there battles where God is calling you to stop striving and rest in the finished victory of Christ?

CHAPTER EIGHT

The Decree of Life

On that day King Ahasuerus gave Queen Esther the house of Haman, the enemy of the Jews. Mordecai came before the king because Esther disclosed who he was to her. ~Esther 8:1

The Transfer of Authority

Coming from the events of chapter 7, the scene opens in the wake of judgment. Haman—the accuser and the architect of death—is removed from the presence of the king and destroyed by the very means he had devised for Mordecai. His own gallows become his sentence, and his own pride becomes his undoing. The text's phrasing, "removed from the presence of the king," carries the gravity of courtroom language. It echoes the earliest exile recorded in Scripture; *"So He drove out the man..." (Genesis 3:24).* To be cast from presence is to be cut off from life itself. It's not simply punishment; it's the natural consequence of rebellion. Sin always ends with separation from the Source.

Yet even as wrath is enacted, Esther—the bride—is pre-served within it. She stands untouched amid judgment, not because she is distant, but because she is beloved. This moment captures the nature of covenant love: it does not exempt the Bride from the scene of judgment, but it preserves her through it. So, her safety is not circumstantial, it's relational. And she is shielded not by escape, but by favor. This distinction lies at the heart of God's justice. Just as Noah was carried through the flood and not around it, Esther remains within the storm of wrath but under the covering of grace.

After these things, the king transfers everything belonging to Haman into Esther's possession. The wealth, the estate, the symbol of dominion, all of it now belongs to the Bride. Yet Esther doesn't hoard the inheritance; she delegates it to Mordecai. The gesture is more than generosity, it's a spiritual pattern in which the favor bestowed upon the Bride is meant to flow outward into the body. So what she receives from the king, she entrusts to another for administration.

This imagery mirrors the spiritual economy of the New Testament. Paul describes in Ephesians 4:7–12 that when Christ ascended, He *"gave gifts to men."* The spoils of His victory became the empowerment of His people. Authority once held by the enemy was stripped away and redistributed to the Church for the work of ministry. In the same way, Esther and Mordecai now share in the king's dominion: one as the crowned Bride, the other as the commissioned servant. But each is reflecting a facet of the redeemed community under God's authority.

So now, both Esther and Mordecai stand as rulers in the king's court, administrators of his will and image-bearers of his authority. It's a scene that resonates through the entire arc of redemption:

"heirs of God, and joint-heirs with Christ" (Romans 8:17). Their exaltation isn't mere promotion, it's typology. The Bride now reigns where accusation once ruled. The kingdom that was once threatened by deception now thrives under delegated righteousness. Revelation 20:6 finds its foreshadow here: *"They shall reign with Him."*

So, what unfolds in this moment is the great exchange of spiritual history. The dominion once wielded by the enemy is disinherited and placed into the hands of the redeemed. The wealth of the wicked, as Proverbs foretold, is laid up for the righteous.

This is also a turning point where Esther's story shifts from deliverance to dominion, and from survival to sovereignty. The war has been won, but now comes the stewardship of victory.

Here, we can see the progression revealed in this transition:

- Haman's removal — the defeat of sin and Satan.
- Esther's protection — the preservation of the Bride within God's wrath.
- Inheritance transfer — the justification and empowerment of the redeemed.
- Delegation to Mordecai — the distribution of Christ's authority to His body.

So, what began as a narrative of rescue now becomes one of reign. And the Bride steps forward not as a survivor of judgment, but as a co-heir in the King's covenant. The decree of death has been overturned, and the scepter of life now rests in her hands.

The Posture of Intercession

Then notice how Esther humbles herself before the king and pleads on behalf of her people. This is a picture of power descending into humility, and authority expressed through surrender. Only a chapter ago, she was standing in uncertainty, yet now she stands adorned with royal favor, possessing wealth, authority, and the full trust of the king. And yet her first act after elevation is to bow lower. That inversion mirrors the very character of Christ.

> *"Who, being in the form of God, did not consider equality with God something to be grasped, but made Himself of no reputation... He humbled Himself and became obedient unto death." ~Philippians 2:6–8*

In Esther, the crown kneels and glory descends. Her favor bends low to intercede for those still condemned. That is not weakness, it is the mystery of holy strength. The paradox of spiritual power then is that true authority never exerts dominance; it intercedes. The crown on her head does not distance her from the people. Instead, it draws her nearer to their suffering. She bows not because she must, but because love compels her to.

And yet she remains human, still trembling before the throne, with her courage still mingled with fear. This is also the culmination of her spiritual arc, and the fruit of all that has come before this moment. The young woman who once uttered, "If I perish, I perish," now stands in full spiritual maturity. Her faith is no longer reactive (born from crisis), but proactive (rooted in conviction).

The refining of her obedience has birthed the fullness of her calling.

This is the same pattern God has always used to form His saints, like Abraham waiting decades for the promise, Moses shaped in the solitude of the wilderness, and David trained in exile before his throne. Faith matures most naturally through seasons of process. So, Esther's elevation is not the end of her journey, but the moment her faith blossoms into its purpose.

And now her voice carries anointing. Here, she actively intercedes for her people. She stands before the king, embodying the very ministry that Christ Himself fulfills eternally.

"He ever lives to make intercession for them."
~Hebrews 7:25

So, Esther's role becomes a reflection of that heavenly reality. She pleads, but cannot repeal, and she intercedes, but cannot redeem. The narrative makes it clear that justice cannot simply be undone. The decree written by the king cannot be revoked, just as God's cannot be erased. His righteousness demands consistency, and His justice cannot contradict His nature.

To simply make sin disappear would be to compromise holiness itself. Thus, Esther's appeal mirrors the tension of God's justice in which the decree remains, but mercy seeks a way through it. In other words, God does not ignore sin; He absorbs it.

So the irreversible decree stands, yet another decree is prepared to supersede it. The first speaks of death while the second declares life. This dual reality — the coexistence of judgment and grace — finds its ultimate fulfillment in Christ.

"For the law of the Spirit of life in Christ Jesus has set you free from the law of sin and death." ~Romans 8:2

So, where Esther intercedes, Jesus intervenes. And where she pleads for reversal, He becomes the reversal. He satisfies justice not by canceling the decree, but by carrying its sentence upon Himself. That's the mystery of the Cross in which judgment is met and mercy is made manifest in the same moment.

This moment also continues the symbolism that runs through the book in which Esther and Mordecai together represent the believer, or more broadly, the Body of Christ.

Their dual roles depict salvation as both relational and functional.

- Esther embodies communion and intimacy — the Bride before the King, resting in favor and interceding in love.

- Mordecai embodies vocation and representation — the servant-leader before the world, administering righteousness and decree.

Together, they form a living portrait of the Church: beloved and commissioned, seated with Christ in heavenly places yet sent into the world to declare His decree. Their relationship also mirrors the Church's twofold life through contemplation and mission, prayer and action, devotion and proclamation. It's the same pattern reflected in the early disciples with Mary who sat at His feet, and Peter who carried His word.

Yet the decree still stands for those outside the covenant. The law remains unchanged for those who have not yet received grace. This is the tension that propels both Esther's plea and the Church's mission through the longing to see mercy extended where judgment still looms. Grace received must become grace proclaimed.

In this way, chapter 8 is not merely a post-redemptive moment, it is a missional one. It shows the transition from being saved to becoming sent.

So Esther's intercession now reaches beyond personal deliverance; becomes representative. She stands between the King and those still under decree — an image of the Church standing between heaven and earth, pleading for mercy to reach those yet untouched by grace.

Yet even her compassion has limits. Her love cannot erase what only God can satisfy. This is where the story points forward again to Christ, the one true Mediator.

Throughout Scripture, we see this same pattern repeated:
- Moses intercedes, yet cannot enter the Promised Land.
- David desires to build the temple, yet cannot complete it.
- Esther pleads before the throne, yet cannot nullify the decree.

All are forerunners of the One who would finish what they began.

"For there is one God and one Mediator between God and men — the man Christ Jesus." ~1 Timothy 2:5

Christ alone fulfills what all human intercessors could only foreshadow. He is both Judge and Advocate, the One who bears the law's weight and releases its captives. In Him, righteousness and mercy are no longer at odds; they embrace.

"Mercy and truth have met together; righteousness and peace have kissed." ~Psalm 85:10

This is the mystery now unveiled through Esther's plea that the throne of justice is also the seat of mercy, and the voice that once condemned now calls His Bride by name.

The New Decree

So the story continues, and though the first decree re-mains steadfast, a new decree is written — just as it has been spiritually through Christ. The two edicts that govern Esther's world mirror the two laws that govern redemptive history.

- The first decree (Haman's edict) represents the unchangeable justice of God — the spiritual law of sin and death (Romans 8:2). It stands as a legal reflection of God's holiness. The decree cannot be revoked because God's justice cannot be compromised.

- The second decree (Mordecai's edict) represents the redemptive counter-law — the law of the Spirit of life through Christ Jesus. It doesn't cancel the first; it conquers it through fulfillment.

Both coexist together through judgment and mercy, law and life, holiness and grace. This is why Jesus declared in *Matthew 5:17, "I have not come to abolish the law, but to fulfill it."* God's justice remains intact, but its power to condemn is neutralized through the cross. The wrath that once hung over humanity now finds resolution in the One who bore it.

So the decree of death still stands, but a new decree now overrides its power. And the same King who once permitted judgment now authorizes redemption through the mediation of His appointed servant.

And note the "coincidental" timing: Mordecai writes the new edict on the 23rd day of the third month which is the month of Sivan. That single detail is far from incidental. Sivan corresponds with Shavuot (Pentecost), the feast marking the giving of the Law at Sinai, and, in the New Testament, the outpouring of the Spirit in Acts 2.

This timing transforms Mordecai's decree into a prophetic shadow. It's as if heaven itself is speaking through the text saying, "What was once written on stone is now being written on hearts."

The first covenant was inscribed by the hand of God on Mount Sinai. The new covenant, through the Spirit, is written within the human soul. And in between — here in Esther — we glimpse the transitional image: a royal decree authored by the king's servant, is sealed with the king's authority, and sent to every nation under his rule.

It's a beautiful parallel across redemptive history:

- At Sinai, the Law was written on stone tablets by the hand of God.

- In Susa, the decree of life is written by the hand of Mordecai.

- At Pentecost, the new covenant is written by the Spirit upon human hearts.

Sivan becomes the month of covenant renewal, and is repeated through the ages in which Law, Grace, and Spirit all converge in the same pattern.

The text then draws attention to two actions: the signing and sealing of the decree, and its sending to every province. These are not just bureaucratic details.

1. The Seal — Ownership and Authority

In the Persian kingdom, a decree sealed with the king's ring was irrevocable. The seal declared ownership, and the mark of absolute authority. Once the impression was made in wax, it carried the full weight of the king's will.

In the same way, believers are sealed by the Holy Spirit by the unbreakable mark of God's ownership (Ephesians 1:13). So, just as the king's ring validated Mordecai's decree, the Spirit validates the covenant of Christ within us. The seal means the decree cannot be undone. It is finished.

2. The Sending — The Great Commission

The decree isn't meant for the palace; it's sent into the world. Mordecai's edict is carried on swift horses to every province and translated into every tongue. This is an empire-wide proclamation of deliverance. The text emphasizes urgency: *"The couriers rode out, hurried and pressed on by the king's command."*

This mirrors the gospel itself in which the Word was written, sealed, and sent forth to every nation.

Just as Mordecai's decree reached *"every people and language,"* so the Spirit at Pentecost enabled the apostles to declare the gospel to *"every nation under heaven."* ~*Acts 2:5–6*

It's as if Esther 8 contains a microcosm of Pentecost in which the decree is written, sealed, and sent; carrying the King's authority to bring life to those once appointed for death.

Passover

Then the text marks the date — "on the thirteenth day of the twelfth month, the month of Adar" — the same day Haman's original decree was to be carried out. That date was meant to be a day of destruction; a day when death reigned and the covenant people were doomed.

But now, under the new decree, that very same day becomes the day of deliverance. So the date of death becomes the dawn of redemption. And that reversal is a picture of the gospel:

- The Cross — a day of death — became the day of life.
- The Tomb — a symbol of defeat — became the threshold of resurrection.
- The Decree that condemned — became the decree that justified.
- Even the timing ties back to Passover, the feast of deliverance from death:

- Passover: The blood of the lamb redeems the firstborn from judgment.
- Esther: The decree of the king redeems the people from annihilation.
- Christ: The blood of the Lamb redeems humanity from eternal death.

Each points to the same continuum picture of the covenant of redemption fulfilled through every age, and each time bringing a greater revelation of mercy. So, what was once the day of despair now becomes the day of deliverance and the enemy's calendar has been rewritten.

The Authorization of the Redeemed

Then the decree goes out, and suddenly the powerless are given permission to stand. The Jews throughout the empire are now authorized to defend themselves against any who would attack, and, remarkably, even to plunder the spoils of their enemies.

At first glance, it reads as a legal reversal, and a defensive right granted by royal decree. But beneath the surface, this is far more than an administrative correction.

Up to this point, the covenant people have walked through a threefold pattern:

1. Condemned by decree — bound under the law of sin and death.
2. Delivered through intercession — redeemed by favor and covenant.

3. Commissioned through empowerment — sent forth to stand and overcome.

This is the rhythm of redemption itself, and the believer's spiritual progression from bondage to battle. God doesn't simply rescue His people; He restores their authority. And He doesn't just pull them out of the fire, He crowns them with the right to rule in His name. They move from victims to victors, and from survival to sovereignty.

"Be strong in the Lord and in the power of His might. Put on the full armor of God... that you may stand against the schemes of the devil." ~Ephesians 6:10–13

The Jews' empowerment is not a call to vengeance but a commissioning under covenant protection, and permission to stand in the authority of the King. So this is not just a reaction, it is restoration.

In the ancient world, to "plunder" was the privilege of conquerors and the sign of dominion restored. So when Mordecai's decree allows the Jews to plunder those who attack, it isn't cruelty; it's covenant symbolism and a visible declaration that the authority of the righteous has replaced the dominion of the wicked.

"And the Israelites plundered the Egyptians." ~Exodus 12:36

The wealth of oppression became the inheritance of the redeemed. The oppressor's power was stripped, and the people of God walked out carrying the tokens of victory. It's the fulfillment of Proverbs 13:22:

"The wealth of the wicked is stored up for the righteous."

Spiritually, this corresponds also to Christ's declaration in Luke 11:21–22:

"When a strong man, fully armed, guards his palace... but when someone stronger attacks and overpowers him, he takes away the armor in which the man trusted and divides the spoils."

Christ is that Stronger One. He has overpowered the enemy, stripped his weapons, and divided the spoils, not as plunder for pleasure, but as evidence of His triumph. And the Church, His Body, now walks in that delegated victory. So this moment in Esther doesn't glorify violence, it glorifies justice. The spoils are not trophies of cruelty but testimonies of covenant fulfillment.

The decree then further details the scope of their defense from armies and provinces to families and households, even "women and children." It reveals the total reach of the decreed justice.

Every level of society, every region, and every class are all named. No person or power that aligns itself with evil is exempt from judgment. It's the language of universal authority.

"That at the name of Jesus every knee should bow, in heaven and on earth and under the earth, and every tongue confess that Jesus Christ is Lord." ~Philippians 2:10–11

This is not the partial protection of a privileged few, it is the total preservation of God's covenant people. It mirrors the thoroughness of the Exodus, where not a single Israelite remained bound and not even a hoof was left behind (Exodus 10:26; 12:51).

So in Esther, the same truth holds in that every Jew, from palace to province, stands covered by royal authority. Spiritually, this represents the full scope of Christ's redemptive dominion and the reclamation of creation itself.

Every "class" or "category" of attacker; whether physical, spiritual, or systemic, symbolizes a force of darkness that is now rendered powerless under divine authority. This is cosmic warfare in narrative form. The Bride (Esther) and the righteous witness (Mordecai) now extend their authority through the body — the covenant people — to resist, stand, and overcome.

This passage connects directly to Ephesians 6 and Revelation 12:

- In Ephesians 6, believers are clothed in the armor of God, standing firm against spiritual opposition.
- In Revelation 12, the dragon wages war against *the rest of her offspring — those who keep God's commands and hold fast their testimony.*

Together, these texts reveal the same reality displayed here in which the Bride and her offspring (the covenant people) wage war not by power, but by presence, and not by force, but by faith. And crucially, the authority exercised by the people does not originate from them, but it flows through them. In other words, they are not the source of power, but its stewards. So their strength is derivative, not inherent. It is the extension of the King's decree through His body, just as Christ's authority flows through His Church.

Macro Implications

This section of the text represents the ecclesiological turning point of Esther's story. It's where the narrative shifts from personal redemption to corporate participation, from royal courts to the vast empire. And the favor that once covered an individual now covers a people.

The people of God, once silenced under threat, now walk in delegated authority. They are empowered, not exempt, and engaged in warfare, not withdrawn from it. They are protected, yet purposed to fight.

This is the same reality that defines the Church today. We are redeemed by grace, sealed by the Spirit, and sent to stand against the darkness of the age. The people of Esther's day rise in royal commission while the people of Christ rise in divine authority.

And in both, the same message resounds that redemption is never passive, it is participatory.

Word and Witness in Motion

Notice also, how the king's new decree does not linger. It is not meant to remain within the walls of the palace, admired as a document of royal wisdom. The text says it is sent out with haste, a phrase loaded with both urgency and obedience. What the king has spoken must now be carried to every province, every people, and every tongue. The decree of life cannot remain still.

That word haste carries weight also. It is not anxiety or chaos, it is immediacy. Throughout Scripture, when God speaks, His word moves. Creation itself was born in haste, "And God said... and it was so." The prophets delivered their oracles in fire and thunder, not delay. When the angel tells the women at the tomb, *"Go quickly and tell His disciples,"* It is the same principle: what heaven decrees must be proclaimed without hesitation.

"So shall My word be that goes forth from My mouth; it shall not return to Me void, but it shall accomplish what I please."
~Isaiah 55:11

Mordecai, now operating under royal authority, becomes the vessel of that word. But his haste is not human ambition; it is obedience to the King's will. So the message is clear: once the decree of life is issued, the only fitting response is to carry it forth. This reflects the same spiritual rhythm that drives the Church's mission. The gospel, once entrusted to us, is not meant to be pondered in private halls, instead, it must run.

"The word of the Lord spread through the whole region."
~Acts 13:49

The "swift horses" and "royal messengers" of Esther 8 find their New Testament parallel in the apostles and disciples who carried the news of Christ to every nation.

In this sense, Mordecai stands as a living type of the apostolic Church; sent out from the presence of the King, bearing His authority, and carrying His decree of life into a world still shadowed by the old law of death. The written decree then becomes word in motion, and the once-mournful servant becomes a witness in power.

So where Mordecai once stood outside the gate in sackcloth and ashes, barred from the palace and broken in spirit, he now emerges from the throne room crowned, robed, and radiant. The transformation is amazing. What was humiliation has become honor, and what was exclusion has become exaltation.

So we can see that this is much more than just narrative symmetry, it is a portrait of resurrection. The man who could not enter the gate now walks out of the palace as a reflection of the king's own glory. His change of garments signals far more than political promotion; it is covenantal transformation.

He enters in his own clothes; a symbol of human limitation, of righteousness that could not stand in the King's presence. Yet he leaves clothed and crowned in the garments of another, a sign of imputed righteousness and restored relationship.

"He has clothed me with the garments of salvation, He has covered me with the robe of righteousness." ~Isaiah 61:10

This is the believer's exchange by symbolism through the moment when our rags of striving are replaced by the robes of grace. The crown upon Mordecai's head represents delegated authority, the same way Christ declares of His Church, *"I have given you authority." (Luke 10:19)*

The robe, the crown, and the restored presence, each tell a part of the same story: justification, sanctification, and glorification.

The Bride and the Witness Aligned

Isaiah 61 and Revelation 19 frame this image on both ends of redemption history. In Isaiah, the individual rejoices— *"He has clothed me."* In Revelation, the collective Bride shines— *"She was given fine linen, bright and pure."*

Mordecai embodies both movements: an individual redeemed who now represents a people restored. His personal righteousness mirrors the Church's corporate glory. And the single servant now foreshadows the radiant multitude.

The story has moved from ashes to beauty (Isaiah 61:3), from humility to exaltation (Philippians 2:9), and from servant to co-heir (Romans 8:17). So what was hidden at the gate is now displayed before the empire. And what was silent intercession becomes public vindication.

"When Christ, who is your life, appears, then you also will appear with Him in glory." ~Colossians 3:4

Mordecai's emergence from the throne room is a glimpse of that future unveiling. The world that once dismissed him now beholds his glory; not his own, but that of the King reflected through him.

The hidden faithful, clothed in humility, will one day be revealed in splendor before all nations. This is not fiction, it is eschatology in narrative form. Mordecai's transformation is the gospel's endgame in which humanity is restored, radiant in righteousness, and bearing the image and authority of the true King.

The Joy of Redemption

So, when the decree of life goes forth, the text says that "the Jews celebrated, and the city of Susa shouted with joy."

This is more than civic relief or political victory. It is the first time in the book that joy bursts beyond the palace walls. Up until now, every act of courage or faith—Esther's fast, Mordecai's lament, the king's favor—has been confined to private spaces. But now the covenant blessing breaks containment and it spills out into the streets.

The joy of the Jews in Susa is not ordinary happiness, but the public manifestation of divine reversal. The same city that once stood in confusion under Haman's edict (Esther 3:15) now resounds with light and gladness under Mordecai's. The writer intentionally contrasts the two scenes:

"The city of Susa was bewildered." (Esther 3:15)

"The city of Susa shouted and rejoiced." (Esther 8:15)

Between those two verses lies the entire gospel pattern in which darkness turned to light, mourning into music, and death into deliverance.

"You turned my mourning into dancing; You removed my sackcloth and clothed me with joy." ~Psalm 30:11

So what began as sackcloth and silence now becomes song and radiance. This is what salvation looks like when it reaches its corporate expression, and when the inner work of redemption becomes an outward festival.

Spiritually, this mirrors the joy of the early Church after the resurrection. The same people who had wept at the cross were found *"rejoicing continually in the temple" (Luke 24:52-53)* once the Spirit was poured out. The news of life could not be contained; it reverberated from upper rooms to city streets. In that sense, Esther 8:15–17 is the Pentecost of Persia. The decree of life has been written, sealed, and sent, and now it ignites collective rejoicing across the nations.

The Fear That Draws

Then comes one of the most surprising verses in the chapter:

"Many of the people of the land professed to be Jews, because the dread of the Jews had fallen on them." ~Esther 8:17

At first glance, it seems like mass fear. But the Hebrew word *pachad* conveys not only terror, but awe, a trembling recognition of holiness. What the Persians witness is not military dominance, but unmistakable divine favor. The covenant is visible, and its gravity pulls even outsiders toward it.

In a polytheistic empire, to identify with the Jews was a radical act. Aligning with God's people could cost one's position, reputation, and even life. And yet they professed and they declared allegiance to the very God whose name is never written in the book but whose hand directs every page.

"In those days ten men from every nation will take hold of the hem of one Jew's robe and say, 'Let us go with you, for we have heard that God is with you.'" ~Zechariah 8:23

"Nations will come to your light, and kings to the brightness of your dawn." ~Isaiah 60:3

What happens in Susa is just a small portrait of that prophecy fulfilled in which the nations are drawn not by argument, but by awe. They don't share the bloodline, but they step beneath the same decree of life.

Grafted by Grace

This moment foreshadows the mystery Paul describes in Romans 11:17–18: *"You, though a wild olive shoot, have been grafted in among the others and now share in the nourishing sap from the olive root."*

The Persians who "professed to be Jews" stand as an Old Testament shadow of the Gentiles grafted into the covenant. They are drawn not by compulsion but by recognition, and by seeing the power of God active among His people and desiring to be part of it.

So the irony once again is revealed in which the empire that once decreed death upon the Jews now sees its own citizens joining them for life. The oppressor becomes the con-vert, judgment turns to invitation, and fear becomes evangelism.

But it's important to note that this is not evangelism by persuasion, it is evangelism by revelation. When God's favor is displayed so undeniably that even unbelievers tremble, hearts turn without debate. The "fear of the Jews" mirrors the "fear of the Lord" revealed by a holy reverence that leads to life.

Acts 5:11 describes a similar moment after Ananias and Sapphira: *"Great fear came upon the whole church and all who heard these things."*

And what followed? The Church multiplied. That same paradox unfolds here in Persia in which holy dread births holy devotion. It is the magnetism of glory and divine power so evident that it draws nations like iron to light.

The Song of Salvation

So now we see that the progression of Esther 8 mirrors the entire arc of redemptive history:

1. Covenant delivered – the decree of life written and sealed.
2. Authority established – Mordecai robed and crowned in righteous-ness.
3. Word sent forth – the message carried swiftly to every land.
4. Nations drawn in – outsiders aligning with God's people in awe.

It's the same pattern repeated from Genesis to Revelation: promise → fulfillment → proclamation → expansion.

So if Chapter 7 was the Cross, then Chapter 8 is Pentecost—the outpouring of authority, identity, and mission upon the Bride. The law of death has been overcome by the decree of life, and the nations now see and rejoice.

The story that began in silence now ends in song. And the hidden hand of God is no longer hidden, it is revealed through His redeemed people. This is the joy that rings through the streets of Susa and still resounds through the ages in what was once condemned has now been redeemed, and the joy of salvation has gone to the whole world.

Closing Remarks

The beauty of this chapter, in my opinion, lies in the very place where the story began. Within the city where oppression once reigned and corruption seeped through every crack and crevice, redemption was proclaimed victorious. And by no means other than providence itself are the multitudes now singing and shouting in praise.

It is a comfort—this song that reminds us how futile our efforts may be, yet how rewarding the love of a Savior truly is. What no man or earthly king could accomplish, the King of Glory has already fulfilled. And what no decree or edict could set in stone, our hope remains fixed upon the One who is our Chief Cornerstone.

What once began in silence now ends in song, for the King who was hidden has made Himself known.

The very paradox of who Christ is displays His power and majesty in ways that never cease to amaze. We could spend a lifetime searching out the mysteries of that paradox, and it would be a most satisfying and fruitful endeavor.

Reflection and Discussion

1. God often turns the very ground of our pain into the soil of His redemption.

    What would it look like for the "city" of your own sorrow to become the place where His joy breaks forth?

2. The law of sin and death still echoes in the world, yet grace speaks the louder word.

    How deeply have you allowed the decree of life to redefine your identity and silence the old verdict that once accused you?

3. The King's decree was sealed long before it was seen.

    In what areas of your life are you still waiting for the visible to catch up to what has already been spoken in heaven?

4. The people of Susa rejoiced not because their world was safe, but because their God was near.

    When was the last time your joy sprang not from circum-stance, but from revelation, from seeing God's hand where once there was silence?

5. Many professed faith not out of persuasion, but awe, because divine favor became undeniable.

    Does your life carry that same evidence cf God's presence, so unmistakable that even those who do not yet believe are moved to wonder.

CHAPTER NINE

The Rise of the Redeemed

...When the king's edict and his decree were to be carried out on the day that the enemies of the Jews had hoped to have power over them, things were turned around. The Jews gained power over those who hated them. ~Esther 9:1

The Decree of Dominion

The narrative of chapter 9 opens in a moment of transition. Notice how what began in Esther 3 as ink on parchment now moves into power and action. The words once sealed by the king's signet have crossed the threshold from written permission to living authority. So the Jews are no longer cowering under the shadow of survival, they are standing in the light of empowerment.

This moment marks the spiritual shift from deliverance to dominion. The people of God move from defense to declaration and from pleading to possessing. The decree of life then becomes a visible emblem of spiritual commission, and what was once merely permission to defend themselves now becomes empowerment to act within the will of the king.

It's the same transformation that occurs in the believer's walk. There comes a point when faith ceases to be a desperate grasp for rescue and becomes a steady stride in delegated authority. The gospel therefore doesn't leave us at the mercy of circumstance, but rather, it positions us under the authority of Christ to reign through righteousness.

> *"Be strong in the Lord and in the power of His might."*
> *~Ephesians 6:10–13*

Just as the Jews' authority flowed from royal decree, so the believer's authority flows from the cross. But it's important to note that their power was not self-made, it was covenantal. Meaning that it did not originate in ambition, but in alignment. So the difference between Haman's rule and Mordecai's reign is the difference between manipulation and legitimacy in which one grasps for power while the other is entrusted with it.

The Great Reversal

As the story then progresses, the phrase *"the reverse happened"* is meant to stand out to the reader. It is simply stated, but is presented as the theological axis of the entire book of Esther. Everything turns on this hinge of divine reversal in what was meant for destruction becomes deliverance, and what was decreed for death now becomes life. We see this repeated throughout Scripture:

- Joseph, sold into slavery, rises to save his betrayers.

- The Cross, a symbol of execution, becomes the instrument of salvation.
- The Resurrection, the ultimate reversal, transforms finality into victory.

In each, God's justice does not bypass human participation, it redeems it. But the Jews still had to rise and act within the will of the king, just as believers today must enact grace through obedience. In other words, reversal is never passive; it requires response.

The same is true for the Church. We are not autonomous agents of power but authorized representatives of God's will. The Church's authority—meaning the Body of Christ itself, not a denomination—is covenantal, not carnal, and it is rooted in relationship, not rank. We act not by self-exaltation, but by reflection of the King's decree.

The Dread of the Righteous

"No man could stand against them, for the dread of them had fallen on all people." ~ Esther 9:2

This moment stands in direct contrast to the fear de-scribed in the previous chapter. In Esther 8, the "fear of the Jews" fell upon the people in such a way that many through-out the empire joined themselves to them. That fear was reverent through recognition of the unmistakable hand of God upon the Jews and desired to share in their covering. It was the awe that draws rather than repels.

But here, in chapter 9, that same supernatural presence produces an entirely different kind of fear—the dread of the enemy. The tone shifts from reverence to resistance collapsing. So now those who once hated the Jews now tremble before them. It's the same pattern we see that when God's favor rests on His people, the world responds either in reverence or in dread.

"No one shall stand against you; the Lord your God will lay the fear of you upon all the land." ~Deuteronomy 11:25

The difference lies in posture. The humble are drawn near; the proud are driven back. Those who recognize the hand of God seek refuge beneath it, while those who oppose it are crushed by its weight.

So the "dread" that falls upon the Persians here is not ordinary fear. The same power that once drew outsiders to the covenant now disarms its enemies. And it is revealed that God's justice works on both sides of the equation: mercy to the repentant, and terror to the rebellious.

This is what happens when light enters territory long ruled by darkness. The atmosphere itself changes. The fear that once bound God's people now binds their oppressors. And the decree of life becomes a banner of holy dread through a reminder that God's justice doesn't simply react to evil, it overturns it. So where His hand rests in favor, no adversary can stand against it.

The Fear of Mordecai

"Even those in authority helped the Jews, because the fear of Mordecai had fallen upon them." ~Esther 9:3

216

This verse reveals how the influence of one righteous man reshaped an empire. Mordecai, once a marginal figure at the gate, now stands as the visible vessel of royal will. He functions here as a Christ-figure bearing delegated power, executing righteous decree, and inspiring reverence not through force, but through favor.

Righteous authority compels cooperation, not coercion. And such legitimacy magnetizes even secular structures toward justice. This is the moral architecture of the Kingdom in which God exalts those who walk in integrity, and their influence becomes gravitational.

So Mordecai's rise is not political opportunism, it is spiritual order. When righteousness governs, even the powers of the world are drawn into alignment. The same principle applies in every age by which God's anointed representatives become conduits of His authority, shaping nations not by might, but by the quiet weight of spiritual credibility.

The Growth of True Authority

"Mordecai had written under the authority of the king... and his power grew more powerful." ~Esther 9:4

This single line captures the nature of godly stewardship. The more Mordecai exercised the authority entrusted to him, the more it multiplied. It is the law of faithful increase, and what Jesus described when He said, *"To everyone who has, more will be given."* *(Luke 19:26)*

True authority expands not through ambition, but through obedience. It grows organically from righteousness, not from reputation. Haman's influence had to be manipulated, sustained by flattery and fear. But Mordecai's needed no such scaffolding; it flowed naturally from alignment with the king's will.

This displays a stark contrast: coercion versus covenant, and fear of man versus fear of God. Dominion born of pride collapses under its own weight, but authority rooted in righteousness endures and multiplies. So Mordecai's power was not about domination, it was about representation. His rise mirrors the believer's own calling: to walk in the King's authority, reflect His justice, and rule with humility under His decree.

The Day of Fulfillment

The narrative now shifts from when the moment of authorization has passed to when the day of execution arrives. "Then the Jews gathered themselves together... and no one could withstand them." The verbs here—gathered, rose up, struck down—signal movement from permission to participation. And what began as a royal decree written in the king's court now unfolds through the hands of the covenant people.

However, this movement is not random violence; it is a response to their commission. The people act not out of vengeance, but in alignment with their given authority. It's a picture of faith in motion and of grace translated into obedience. In the same way, spiritual authority in the life of a believer demands cooperation, not passivity. The decree of God's Word must be enacted by faith.

As the body without the Spirit is dead, so faith without works is dead," ~James 2:26

"Therefore take up the whole armor of God that you may be able to resist in the evil day, and having done all, to stand."
~Ephesians 6:13

Thus, grace does not excuse inaction, it commissions action. It moves the redeemed from survival to stewardship, from fear to faith, and from defense to dominion. The Jews are no longer cowering under threat; they now advance under favor. The same is true for the Church today. Spiritual maturity begins when believers stop living reactively and start walking proactively under Christ's authority.

The Exposure of Hostility

The text then tells us that in the city of Susa alone, 500 people were killed—those who "hated the Jews." So the decree didn't erase hostility, it exposed it. Evil, when confronted by God's order, is then forced into visibility. And those who had harbored hatred in silence now reveal themselves in open rebellion.

This moment echoes a broader message in that even after Christ's victory on the Cross, opposition still rises. The gospel does not remove conflict, it defines it. The decree of grace exposes rebellion before it destroys it. And the enemy's final resistance is often the loudest before it collapses.

These attackers symbolize more than historical adversaries; they represent the spiritual forces that still oppose God's people through sin, deception, pride, and unbelief. The Jews' active stance here then becomes a metaphor for spiritual posture. We are not called to live in defensive fear but in offensive faith by standing firm, resisting evil, and advancing the Kingdom under divine authority.

The Death of Haman's Sons

Among those slain were Haman's ten sons. But their deaths are more than a footnote, they carry deep symbolic weight. In Persian culture, having many sons was a mark of prestige, yet the very thing that once represented Haman's pride now becomes the emblem of his fall. The number ten itself carries consistent biblical significance through divine order, human responsibility, and judgment.

- Ten Commandments — the measure of moral responsibility.
- Ten Plagues of Egypt — the full measure of God's judgment.
- Ten Virgins — the testing of readiness and faithfulness.

In this way, Haman's ten sons represent the complete fulfillment of judgment against the Amalekite line and thus the total collapse of rebellion against spiritual order. Their individual names are recorded not as redundancy but as finality. To name is to acknowledge, and to blot out is to erase remembrance. God records righteousness for remembrance and rebellion for removal.

"I will utterly blot out the remembrance of Amalek from under heaven." ~Exodus 17:14

This passage thus closes a generational cycle. The first Amalekite attack against Israel began in Exodus and the last is extinguished here in Esther. So what Saul failed to complete in 1 Samuel 15, Mordecai's generation fulfills it through obedience. The Amalekite line, symbolic of continual enmity against God's people, is finally silenced.

The Spirit of the Defeated

Yet the text invites us to imagine these ten sons, not only as men, but as remnants of a spirit unwilling to surrender. Having lost their father, their status, and their power, they lash out in one last act of hatred. Their rebellion mirrors the pattern of fallen powers described in Revelation 12:12: *"The devil has come down to you in great wrath, because he knows that his time is short."*

This is what the Amalekite spirit represents—pride that refuses repentance even in defeat. It's the shadow of every rebellion that continues to resist the reign of God. Their destruction, then, is not vengeance, it is cleansing. It is God's order being reestablished where chaos once ruled.

Victory Without Corruption

One of the most profound details in this passage is what the Jews do not do. Though they were given permission by royal decree to plunder their enemies, they abstained. Three times the text emphasizes this restraint.

Their refusal to take spoils mirrors Abraham's refusal to accept wealth from the king of Sodom (Genesis 14:23) and stands in stark contrast to Saul's disobedience when he spared Agag and kept the plunder (1 Samuel 15). This time, Israel gets it right.

Victory without greed reveals covenant maturity. The Jews' restraint shows they are no longer fighting for survival or gain, but for righteousness. Their obedience closes the spiritual loop left open generations earlier, and the war against Amalek that once ended in compromise now ends in faith-fulness.

This is holiness in triumph in which power is exercised without corruption and victory is held with humility.

The King's Vindication

When the reports return to the king, his reaction reveals a striking transformation. Earlier in the story, Ahasuerus was a passive figure; easily swayed by counselors, and reacting rather than ruling. But here, something shifts. He's no longer detached or uncertain; he's engaged. The text suggests genuine satisfaction as he learns of the Jews' victory and the judgment carried out on their enemies. His response marks the turning point from hesitation to partnership, and from being a monarch influenced by others to one actively defending justice.

But this is not bloodlust, it's the satisfaction of righteous order restored. The king's zeal mirrors spiritual vindication, the way Scripture describes God's own justice being *"established in righteousness" (Psalm 9:7–8).* The earthly throne in Susa then becomes a shadow of the heavenly one in which both are executing judgment on behalf of the covenant people. So wrath here is not rage; it's resolution. It is justice carried to its fulfillment, and echoes that line once spoken on the cross saying, "It is finished."

So more than just signing the decree, the king becomes its champion, standing in full advocacy of his bride. This moment completes the transformation of the King–Bride relationship. Where Esther once trembled before the throne, she now moves in its confidence. What began as intercession has become partnership, and what began with risk has matured into reign. It's a living picture of Ephesians 5 and Rev-elation 19—where the Bride (the Church) no longer stands in fear of rejection but moves under the protection and authority of her Bridegroom (Christ).

Earlier, Esther risked death to draw near to the throne. Now the throne moves on her behalf. This is the very rhythm of God's favor in which it begins with access and ends with shared authority.

The Continuation of Justice

Esther's next act might seem bold—perhaps even unsett-ling—but it reveals her discernment rather than defiance. When she petitions the king to extend the decree one more day in Susa, she isn't seeking vengeance; she's ensuring completion. So the con-tinuation isn't excess, it's fulfillment.

Throughout Scripture, God's judgment runs to its full course before peace is restored. In other words, His decrees are never partial; they are complete.

"He who began a good work in you will complete it until the day of Jesus Christ." ~Philippians 1:6

So Esther's request follows this same pattern. The work of justice must reach its conclusion so that no remnant of rebellion remains. Her boldness is not born from pride but from prophetic awareness of timing. Esther senses that unfinished judgment leaves room for future threat. Spiritually speaking, this mirrors God's own pattern of sanctification and the continual refining until all that opposes His nature is purged.

The Hanging of Haman's Ten Sons

Then comes her final, striking request: that Haman's ten sons—already dead—be hung upon the gallows. Historically, this would have been a public display of justice, and a visible statement of finality. But spiritually, it's much more than symbolism. It's what Scripture often calls a sign-act, or an enacted parable.

This is not cruelty; it is proclamation. Evil is not just defeated here, it is displayed as conquered. Esther's request parallels the spiritual reality Paul describes in Colossians 2:15: *"He disarmed the rulers and authorities and made a public spectacle of them, triumphing over them in it."*

What happens on the gallows mirrors what happens at the Cross in which judgment was made visible, rebellion was shamed openly, and righteousness was exalted before all creation.

Thus both Haman's and his sons' display carry cosmic implications. Together, they form the visible witness that evil's line has ended. And what was hidden in schemes and darkness is now exposed beneath the light of justice.

The Prototype of the Final Adversary

All of this reinforces Haman's role throughout the book as the archetype of the adversary, and the seed of the serpent introduced in Genesis 3:15. His story is the earthly picture of the cosmic rebellion between the serpent's offspring and the covenant people. And as with all typology in Scripture, his fall prefigures something greater—the ultimate defeat of the antichrist system in Revelation.

- Flattery and manipulation → political seduction (Daniel 11:32)
- Global annihilation intent → persecution of the saints (Revelation 13:7)
- Borrowed authority → counterfeit kingship (Revelation 13:2)
- Self-inflicted destruction → pride turned judgment (Proverbs 16:18)

The parallel is deliberate. Just as Haman rose through borrowed power—the king's ring—so too does the beast of Revelation rule through a borrowed hour. Both operate under temporary permission, and both are overthrown by God's decree.

Haman's ten sons, then, stand as the earthly foreshadowing of the ten kings of Revelation 17:12–14. Both sets represent the complete manifestation of rebellion, and the tenfold defiance unified under a single wicked head. Both rise in collective opposition to God's covenant people. And both are publicly destroyed in righteous reversal.

The pattern is identical:

Ten allied under one head → war → reversal → destruction.

Evil always unites for a season, but its unity becomes its undoing. And the kingdom of darkness inevitably collapses under the weight of God's sovereignty.

The Public Display of Triumph

Thus, Esther's posthumous request to hang the ten sons is meant to serve as a visible declaration that the line of rebellion is over. And what was once a private war has become a public testimony of victory.

This is the essence of righteous triumph. Evil is not merely defeated in secret, it is paraded as powerless. The gallows become the stage of revelation where hidden justice is made visible to every realm—human and spiritual.

So, in Esther's day, this act spoke to the empire: "The decree of death has been overturned and the covenant people stand."

In Christ's fulfillment, the Cross declares the same mess-age to all creation: "Death is defeated and the Kingdom stands forever."

From Battle to Rest

The narrative now enters its final transition through the shift from war to worship, and from decree to remembrance. The fighting ceases, and the text notes something interesting: *"some rested, while others continued to fight."* Not all rested at once. The victory was sure, but its outworking came in stages.

This staggered rest mirrors the very structure of redemption itself—the already and not yet fulfillment of God's promise. The decree had secured deliverance, but its effects were still unfolding. Some tasted peace early while others pressed on until every trace of opposition was removed. It's a picture of the believer's journey in which the war is won through the Cross, yet battles remain until final peace is revealed.

"There remains therefore a rest for the people of God."
~Hebrews 4:9

We live between victory and vigilance. We are redeemed, yet still contending. The Jews' rest in Susa becomes a prophetic image of that future Sabbath rest, when every enemy is finally subdued, and the people of God can lay down their arms in eternal peace.

The Transition from War to Worship

So when the fighting ends, the people rest, and their rest gives birth to celebration. The text says their sorrow was "turned to joy and their mourning into gladness." This is not mere relief; it is worship born out of deliverance.

Rest here then becomes more than the absence of conflict, it becomes the presence of covenant peace. This moment reflects the same pattern seen in Revelation 15, where the saints who overcome the beast stand upon the sea of glass, *"singing the song of Moses and of the Lamb."* Therefore the proper response to victory is not triumphalism but gratitude in which redemption always ends in praise.

The Birth of Purim: From Fear to Feast

From this joy emerges a new celebration—the Feast of Purim. What was once a day of dread now becomes a day of remembrance. The word Purim (from pur, meaning "lot") transforms the symbol of death's decree into a memorial of deliverance. The casting of lots by Haman now becomes the casting of joy by God.

Mordecai formalizes this moment so that future generations will never forget that sorrow has become joy, fear has become feasting, and death has given way to life.

> *"You have turned my mourning into dancing; You have taken off my sackcloth and clothed me with joy." ~Psalm 30:11*

Purim thus joins the great covenant celebrations of Scripture like Passover, the Lord's Supper, and every act of remembrance where God's people pause to recall redemption. So Mordecai's decree, *"that these days should be remembered and kept,"* anticipates Jesus' own words at the table: *"Do this in remembrance of Me."*

Deliverance thus always leads to commemoration, and what God finishes in history, His people preserve in memory.

Joy Overflowing into Generosity

And as part of that celebration, the people exchange gifts and share portions with the poor so that no one is left out. This detail reveals the ethical fruit of redemption by joy that overflows into generosity. True victory produces compassion, not exclusivity.

"Go your way, eat the fat and drink the sweet, and send portions to those for whom nothing is prepared." ~Nehemiah 8:10

The feast becomes a living expression of love, and redemption turned outward. So the covenant community rejoices not in isolation, but in inclusion. In this, joy becomes justice, and fellowship becomes worship.

The text then describes how the celebration spread from Susa—the royal center—to the outer provinces of the empire. This outward movement reveals that the joy of redemption radiates from the heart to the edges, from palace to village, and from the covenant center to distant lands.

And this pattern mirrors the gospel's own trajectory in which salvation begins in Jerusalem and extends to the ends of the earth (Acts 1:8). Therefore redemption is never static, it moves outward until all are invited to the feast. So grace starts in the throne room and flows to the farthest borders of all of creation.

Written in the Book

Finally, the chapter closes with the phrase, *"And it was written in the book."* The circle completes. What began in chapter 6 with the king's sleepless night and the reading of the "book of remembrance" now ends with another record—the book of redemption.

This is more than literary closure; it's theological resolution. The act of writing secures memory in permanence. And the king's record becomes an earthly reminder of the heavenly "Book of Life," where God's covenant victories are eternally inscribed.

Remembrance here then becomes an act of warfare against forgetfulness. What is written cannot be undone, and what God remembers cannot be erased. The book stands as both archive and testimony of history preserved and as prophecy fulfilled.

So, Chapter 9 brings Esther's story to its crescendo in which the decree is fulfilled, the enemies are silenced, and the people rest in joy. What began in hiddenness ends in proclamation. And the mourning of chapter 4 becomes the music of chapter 9.

And in the end, the victory is written, not only in a royal record, but in the eternal memory of God, who turns every decree of death into a decree of redemption.

CLOSING REMARKS

This chapter continues the theme that began in chapter 8—authority. From the moment Esther stepped into the court to touch the scepter of the king until this point, we find that her boldness and authority continue to grow as the forces of evil are simultaneously crushed underfoot. What grace paved the way for, faith is emboldened by.

Time and time again, the reader is reminded that God is consistent in His character and, therefore, in His covenant promise. His name may not be mentioned, yet it resounds unmistakably through every page of this story. And what's more magnificent is the portrait of redemption history revealed through the pattern of His saving grace.

It is always God who extends His favor for us to take hold of, yet He asks that we merely take that first step in surrender. With every hesitant step, He sees boldness taking root and cultivates faith to make us bolder still. And furthermore, He invites us to take part in the work of His glory as He extends His authority through His own bride.

What is evident through our weakness, He fills up with His strength. Our orphaned heritage has been translated into an inheritance in Him with a name to call our own and a crown of splendor upon our heads. Yet the assurance remains that what He has begun in us will be continued until the day of His return. And so, we wait and rest in the wondrous works of His righteousness.

Such rest then leads to celebration and commemoration that invite others to take part as well. We stand no longer plagued by the need to survive, but in victory—commissioned with all authority to move and act in His holy name. For though the rest is good, the day is short, and while the harvest is plenty, the laborers are few.

REFLECTION & DISCUSSION

1. The fear of the righteous terrifies darkness because it mirrors God's order.

   What would change in your life if you fully believed that holiness itself carries a spiritual weight that disarms the enemy?

2. To bring something into the light is to agree with Heaven's verdict over it.

   What stronghold or memory are you still protecting that God has already judged and wants to display as defeated?

3. The measure of victory is not what is gained, but what is willingly surrendered.

   How might choosing not to grasp what you've been "allowed" to take become your most powerful act of worship?

4. Remembrance sanctifies history and it turns pain into redemption.

   What past wound or season could become an altar of remembrance if you allowed gratitude to reinterpret it through redemption?

5. The recording of redemption is not for nostalgia but for witness.

   If your life were inscribed in the book of remembrance, what would it testify about the faithfulness of God through your obedience?

CHAPTER TEN

Redemption Remembered

All the deeds of his power and of his might, and the detailed record of the greatness of Mordecai, after the king Promoted him, are they not written in the book of the chronicles of the kings of Media and Persia? ~Esther 10:2

In this brief epilogue, the narrative shifts from conflict to closure. The text notes that the king imposed a tax on both the land and the coastal regions, reaching across every border of his empire. This decree, though administrative in tone, may serve a dual purpose. First, to refill the royal treasury that Haman once promised to fund through his plot against the Jews, and second, to reestablish the census of the empire's citizens following the defeat of their enemies.

So, the war has ended. Order is restored. And remembrance seals the story.

The human narrative now moves forward, but the spiritual record remains, preserved for all generations to read. This closing chapter, though short, functions as far more than a historical footnote. It brings resolution to the events that have unfolded, marking them with a sense of permanence and completion. What occurred in Esther's day was not merely a passing moment of deliverance, but a turning point that left an enduring imprint upon the world.

This ending reminds us that God's intervention does not simply erase crisis, it transforms it into legacy. The decree of life continues to reverberate, the covenant people remain established, and the memory of God's hidden faithfulness is forever inscribed in the chronicles of both heaven and earth.

If we step back and trace the entire narrative arc through a lens that reaches beyond the stage and the surface, we begin to see that the book of Esther unfolds as a proto-gospel, and a foreshadowing of redemption. Beneath the royal intrigue and human drama lies the story of restoration, mirroring the believer's own journey from lost identity to covenant inheritance.

This duality—between what is seen and what is unseen— defines the very nature of spiritual reality. We live between two dimensions: the natural and the supernatural, or, as Scripture often describes it, the flesh and the spirit. When Jesus told His followers not to look for a physical kingdom as they expected, but for one that was spiritual in nature, He was calling them to perceive through faith rather than sight. It was a reminder that what appears most tangible to us is often the least eternal, and that an earthly perspective can blind us to spiritual truths. What we glean through natural under-standing may be familiar, but it often limits our ability to harvest what is being offered to us in the spirit.

That same principle is revealed through every page of Esther. Though God's name is never mentioned, His presence saturates the text. His hidden hand guides every coincidence, every reversal, and every act of deliverance. The story, while set on a secular stage, continually invites the reader to look deeper; to see providence beneath politics, grace beneath circum-stance, and God's purpose beneath human choice.

Throughout the book, typological language and symbolic patterns appear again and again, connecting Esther's story to the larger biblical narrative. The unseen God who moves through Persia is the same God who parted the Red Sea, raised dry bones to life, and rolled away the stone. The genre may differ—narrative rather than prophecy, history rather than hymn—but the message remains the same: redemption concealed is still redemption revealed.

What makes Esther even more extraordinary is how its uniqueness operates on both literary and spiritual levels. No other story in the Old Testament paints such a complete picture of the gospel narrative from exile to exaltation, and from decree to deliverance. It is a masterpiece hidden in plain sight, and an entire theology of redemption woven into the fabric of an ancient court tale.

Let us now take a step back and trace that redemptive pattern to summarize the journey we have walked together since chapter one.

The Pattern of Redemption

The book of Esther stands apart within the Hebrew canon as one of the most remarkable portrayals of redemption ever written—not through prophecy or overt covenant language, but through the quiet power of narrative reversal. What the prophets declare in words, Esther demonstrates in motion. Its story carries the full pattern of salvation, tracing the same redemptive arc that runs from Genesis to Revelation.

The pattern begins where every story of redemption begins— with the fall. In Esther, this fall is reflected through Haman's decree of death against the Jews, a shadow of the universal law of sin and condemnation that holds humanity captive. The sentence has been written and destruction is imminent. Yet into this hopelessness enters the next movement: substitution and inter-cession. Esther stands before the king as the mediator of her people, risking her own life to plead for theirs. It is a portrait of Christ's atoning work in which the innocent stands before the throne to intercede on behalf of the guilty.

Then comes judgment. The very gallows Haman built for the righteous becomes the instrument of his own downfall. Here God's justice meets poetic symmetry, reminding us of the truth that God's wrath is not arbitrary but righteous and redemptive. Sin's architect falls upon his own design, just as the power of death collapses under the weight of the cross.

What follows is grace. A new decree is written; one that does not erase the old law but supersedes it. The law of death remains on the record, yet it is fulfilled by a greater decree of life. This is justification in narrative form in which the condemnation stands, but the believer now lives under the authority of a higher covenant.

Empowerment then flows naturally from grace. The Jews are authorized to defend themselves—not as aggressors, but as participants in their own deliverance. So what was once passive survival becomes active faith. This mirrors the sanctified life of believers who, through the Spirit's power, move from mere recipients of grace to ambassadors of it. They are no longer victims of circumstance but vessels of God's strength.

Finally, the story culminates in glorification. Mordecai is exalted, Esther is enthroned, and the enemies of the covenant are silenced. The orphan becomes royalty, and the exile becomes the ruler. What began in hiddenness ends in triumph. This is the believer's destiny; to reign with Christ, clothed in righteousness, at rest from all striving.

In just ten chapters, Esther encapsulates the entire gospel economy—fall, intercession, judgment, grace, empowerment, and victory—all without ever mentioning the name of God. That is the genius of His concealment and revelation in which the God who hides His name in the text reveals His nature through it.

But as the narrative structure reveals the pattern of redemption, so too does Esther's composition unveil its theological brilliance. Beneath its brevity lies a work of mystery and intentional design.

What Makes Esther Unique

Esther also presents one of the most striking paradoxes in all of Scripture through the existence of two decrees: one of death and one of life. This tension between judgment and mercy captures the entire spiritual dilemma of humanity. The first decree cannot be revoked, just as the law cannot be nullified; yet a new decree supersedes it, establishing deliverance without negating justice. In

Esther, judgment is upheld, yet mercy is fulfilled through a perfect reflection of the cross where righteousness and peace meet.

The book also forms a complete typological triad, containing within it the Bride, the Mediator, and the Usurper. Esther, the bride, embodies favor and intercession; Mordecai, the mediator, represents righteousness and advocacy; and Haman, the usurper, personifies rebellion and accusation. Through their interplay, the unseen King—God Himself—emerges as the sovereign over every heart, decree, and destiny. This triad mirrors the narrative of Christ and the Church, where the Bride stands redeemed, the Mediator intercedes, and the Accuser is cast down.

Another aspect that makes Esther exceptional is its portrayal of corporate salvation. Esther's courage does not secure deliverance for herself alone but for her entire people. Her intercession becomes the vessel through which a nation is spared. In this way, the story reflects Christ's own substitutionary act, in which one life is offered for the redemption of many.

Covenant transference also stands at the heart of Esther's conclusion. The inheritance of the enemy—the house, the wealth, the authority once held by Haman—is transferred to Esther and Mordecai. This is not mere political irony; it is theological imagery. The possessions of the wicked are given to the righteous, prefiguring the promise of Romans 8:17: "Heirs of God and co-heirs with Christ." It is a visible sign of what grace accomplishes, and what was once ruled by darkness becomes ruled by light.

Finally, Esther quietly anticipates the mystery of Gentile inclusion. The closing verse of chapter eight tells us that "many from the peoples of the land professed to be Jews," drawn by awe at the hand of God upon His people. This moment foreshadows the grafting in of the nations that Paul later describes in Romans 11. Redemption, once limited to a single people, begins to ripple outward toward all nations, fulfilling the promise made to Abraham that through his seed all the earth would be blessed.

Taken together, these elements make Esther one of the most astonishing works of revelation in Scripture. It functions like a hidden gospel wrapped in Old Testament form through a literary parable of redemption written in exile, veiled beneath royal politics and human circumstance.

In other words, scripture does not progress toward the gospel; it is the gospel, revealed in layers. And Esther stands as one of its most elegant unveilings of how the God who hides His name still writes His story in every line.

The Gospel in Esther's Narrative Arc

So, on the macro scale, the narrative traces the sweeping arc of humanity's restoration from exile to covenant, and from condemnation to glory. Yet within that vast movement, it also captures the micro rhythm of the soul's own transformation through the unfolding of grace in the life of one who is chosen, refined, and commissioned. Beneath the royal intrigue and human decisions lies a unique pattern that mirrors both the redemption of the world and the sanctification of the individual.

Orphaned in Exile — Humanity's Fall

The story begins with an orphan in exile who is displaced, unseen, and nameless. Esther's condition at the opening of the book is not merely circumstantial; it is emblematic of the human

241

soul after the Fall. Like her, humanity exists outside its original home, cut off from covenant and shaped by survival rather than identity. She belongs to no one, yet she is chosen without knowing it. Though her story unfolds in the Persian empire, its spiritual origin begins in Eden's aftermath. Humanity has fallen, but grace is already moving in the shadows to restore what was lost.

Chosen by Grace — Salvation

Esther's rise from obscurity to royalty is not born of pedigree, power, or perfection, it is the result of unmerited favor. She is chosen by grace alone, elevated by a decree she did not initiate and could not earn. Her preparation—washed, perfumed, and clothed—mirrors the process of sanctification in the believer's life. The Spirit, like the attendants who prepared Esther, purifies the Bride for her King. So her ascension to the palace is not a reward for merit but a manifestation of mercy.

"You were washed, you were sanctified, you were justified."
~1 Corinthians 6:11

Hidden Identity — The Believer's Walk of Faith

Once in the palace, Esther conceals her true identity. This hiddenness is not cowardice, it is divine timing. In the same way, believers live with an identity that is real yet unseen, hidden with Christ in God (Colossians 3:3). We are in the world but not of it, called to patience while revelation ripens. God often conceals His purposes until the appointed time, and Esther's hidden name becomes a living parable of faith that waits for the ultimate unveiling. So her silence is not absence, it is preparation.

Intercession and Conflict — Spiritual Warfare

The story's turning point begins when Mordecai calls Esther to intercede for her people. Here, the narrative shifts from salvation received to mission embraced. Esther steps into the tension of faith and fear, learning to approach the throne not with entitlement but with surrender. Her fasting and prayer symbolize the believer's struggle in spiritual warfare and the courage to stand in the gap between destruction and deliverance. Like Christ, she becomes an intercessor, risking every-thing so that others might live. Hebrews reminds us to approach the throne of grace with confidence, and Esther's trembling courage models that invitation.

The Reversal — Redemption

When the king extends his scepter toward Esther, grace meets humility. That single gesture embodies the gospel through favor before merit, and pardon before perfection. The decree of death that once condemned her people remains written, but a greater decree now supersedes it. This is the mystery of redemption in which the law of sin and death remains on record, but its power is nullified by the word of life. The first decree reveals judgment; the second declares mercy.

The Accuser Judged — Victory Over Death

Haman, the Agagite and descendant of Amalek, stands as the personification of the accuser, and the ancient enemy of God's covenant people. His fall mirrors the ultimate defeat of Satan. The very gallows he built for the righteous becomes the instrument of his own demise. The weapon formed against the faithful collapses under God's justice. This is the cross in foreshadowed form. The accuser is silenced before the Bride, and death is swallowed up in victory.

"Now the salvation and the power and the kingdom of our God and the authority of His Christ have come, for the accuser of our brothers has been thrown down... And they overcame him by the blood of the Lamb and by the word of their testimony."
~Revelation 12:10-11

The Bride's Rest — Glorification

By the book's end, the tone shifts from struggle to serenity. The Bride and her people are at rest; Mordecai is exalted to second in command, and the Jews dwell in peace beneath royal favor. This rest is not mere relief, it is glorification. The orphan has become royalty. The exile now reigns beside the king. And what began in obscurity ends in authority. It is the believer's story realized in full, and the battle concludes with celebration, echoing the final rest promised to the saints through the joy of redemption completed.

"Those He justified, He also glorified." ~Romans 8:30

Summary

So, in the end, we can see the entire theology of redemption concealed within Esther's narrative:

- Fall: Orphaned in exile
- Salvation: Chosen by grace

- Sanctification: Hidden identity
- Intercession: The believer's call
- Redemption: The decree reversed
- Victory: The accuser destroyed
- Glorification: Rest in covenant

It's Genesis to Revelation in miniature in which a covenant war is fought and won beneath the surface of a royal court.

What begins as a political drama unfolds into a cosmic narrative through the unseen battle between light and dark-ness, promise and rebellion, death and deliverance. Behind every decree and reversal lies the echo of Eden, the shadow of the cross, and the anticipation of the Kingdom to come. The fall, the promise, the conflict, the atonement, and the final rest are all hidden within this story's corridors. So, Esther's throne room becomes a microcosm of redemptive history where the authority of heaven confronts the schemes of hell through ordinary vessels of faith.

Here, the fate of a people mirrors the fate of creation itself and redeemed not by might, but by mercy. And when the scroll of Esther closes, it leaves us not at an ending, but at a foreshadowing of the greater King, the greater Bride, and the final victory written before the foundation of the world.

CLOSING REMARKS

I think the point remains that we, as believers, are deeply encouraged by the matchless sovereignty of our God and the steadfastness of His character in a world that sways in every direction. While kingdoms rise and fall, His promises stand unshaken. We can rest assured in the victory He has already secured and fulfilled according to His covenant faithfulness.

This is the same reminder Paul gave to the early church of *their blessed hope*, and the same truth that John later expounded upon to strengthen the believers of the first century. Yet the message remains unchanged throughout the ages that the Lamb has conquered, His Kingdom endures, and that same hope still calls to us today.

And yet, even as we behold His revealed works, we are reminded that the depths of His mysteries can never be fully grasped. Still, the invitation remains open to all who hunger enough to search them out. We may lose ourselves in the vastness of His ways, but that is the beauty of His nature—that even when we are lost in the depths of His mystery, we are found safely in the embrace of His grace.

Still, the call persists: to seek Him beyond what our limited understanding can comprehend, and to trust the rev-elation of His Spirit that awaits those willing to step deeper into the unseen. Our intellect and knowledge are good and even necessary gifts, but He desires more than comprehension—He desires communion. He asks for the fullness of both heart and mind, united in pursuit of Him, so that such a search becomes an act of worship itself.

"You will seek Me and find Me when you search for Me with all your heart." ~Jeremiah 29:13

"For the things which are seen are temporary, but the things which are unseen are eternal." ~2 Corinthians 4:18

REFLECTION AND DISCUSSION

1. The story began with exile and ended in exaltation.

   How does this pattern mirror your own spiritual journey from separation to communion with God?

2. The king's final decree echoes through time as both justice and mercy intertwined.

   How does the coexistence of judgment and grace shape your understanding of God's character and His dealings with humanity?

3. Esther disappears from the final lines with her mission complete and her legacy secure.

   Can you find peace in the kind of obedience that may go unmentioned but still moves eternity?

4. The law of death remained written, yet its power was broken.

   How can you live each day in the awareness that Christ has already written a greater decree over your life?

5. Esther's chronicle ends, yet redemption's story does not.

   How will you allow the legacy of this hidden gospel to shape your witness in the unseen battles of your own generation?

AFTERWORD

To whoever has walked these pages with me, thank you.

You have journeyed through the courts of Persia, through silence and sovereignty, and through hiddenness and revelation. My prayer is that this study has stirred something deep within you, not merely for understanding, but for hunger. A hunger to know Jesus more fully, to love His Word more deeply, and to recognize His hand weaving redemption through every detail of your own story.

If these chapters have done anything, may they remind you that Scripture is indeed alive. Every page still breathes the same Spirit that hovered over the waters in Genesis, spoke through the prophets, and now dwells within the hearts of those redeemed by the Lamb. The same God who moved in Esther's day moves still in ours— faithful, steadfast, and sovereign in every place.

My hope is that as you close this book, you do not feel an ending, but an awakening through a renewed desire to search out the mysteries of God and to carry the light of His truth into the world around you. Because this story does not end in Persia. It continues in every heart awakened by grace, in every life yielded to

His call, and in every generation that dares to stand "for such a time as this."

The scepter has been extended.

The Bride is being refined.

And the decree of life still stands.

May the God of all Creation — the great Author of our existence and our hope — lift you up in the light of His countenance and bless you in the path and on the journey that He has entrusted you with.

SCRIPTURE REFERENCES BY CHAPTER

All passages quoted or referenced are from the Modern English Version

CHAPTER ONE

Primary Text

Esther 1:2–9 — The setting in Susa, Ahasuerus's banquet, and Vashti's refusal.

Thematic and Cross-References

Luke 1:52 — "He has brought down the mighty from their thrones and exalted those of humble estate."

Romans 8:13 — "If you live according to the flesh, you will die; but if by the Spirit you put to death the deeds of the body, you will live."

Exodus 14:17–18 — "I will get glory over Pharaoh and all his host, that the Egyptians may know that I am the LORD."

Isaiah 48:11 — "For My own sake, for My own sake, I do it… My glory I will not give to another."

Psalm 31:3 — "For Your name's sake You lead me and guide me."

Psalm 106:8 — "Yet He saved them for His name's sake, that He might make His mighty power known."

Doctrinal and Literary Allusions

Genesis 3:24 — The exile motif; humanity removed from divine presence.

Romans 8:13 — Reiterated in the "Flesh vs. Spirit" contrast.

Exodus 14:17–18; Isaiah 48:11; Psalm 31:3; Psalm 106:8 — Illustrating the "Pride vs. Providence" theme and God's sovereignty over human ambition.

CHAPTER TWO

Primary Text

Esther 2:1–23 — The central passage of study, encompassing Esther's preparation, selection, and Mordecai's loyalty at the gate.

Thematic and Cross-References

1 Samuel 15 — Saul's disobedience and failure to destroy Agag, establishing the ancestral conflict later embodied by Mordecai (descendant of Kish) and Haman (the Agagite).

Genesis 1 — The seven days of creation; reflected symbolically in Esther's seven maidservants and the motif of divine completeness.

Exodus 25:37 — The seven-branched lampstand; symbolizing God's order and spiritual fullness.

Isaiah 11:2 — The sevenfold Spirit of God; parallel to the completeness of divine empowerment surrounding Esther.

Revelation 1:4 — The seven Spirits before the throne; an image of covenant wholeness mirrored in Esther's spiritual preparation.

Ruth 4:1 — The seat of justice at the gate; foreshadowing Mordecai's future role as intercessor and redeemer.

Proverbs 31:23 — The gate as a place of counsel and honor; symbolic of Mordecai's faithfulness and advocacy.

Esther 6:10–12 — Foreshadow: the same gate becomes the site of Mordecai's exaltation — reversal through faith-fulness.

Luke 1:52 — "He has brought down the mighty from their thrones and exalted those of humble estate."

A direct reflection of the contrast between Vashti's fall and Esther's rise.

Philippians 2:6–7 — "Who, being in very nature God... humbled Himself."

Used to illustrate Christlike humility reflected through Esther's posture.

Psalm 112:4 — "Even in darkness, light dawns for the upright."

Applied to Esther's placement in a morally compromised system that God redeems from within.

1 Corinthians 1:27 — "God chose the foolish things of the world to shame the wise."

Highlights God's paradoxical pattern of exalting weak-ness to display strength.

John 4:1–26 — The woman at the well; redemption emerging from scandal.

Luke 5:30–32 — Jesus dining with sinners; holiness trans-forming corruption.

Mark 1:40–45 — Jesus touching the leper; purity over-taking impurity.

Doctrinal and Literary Allusions

The Gate — Threshold between judgment and redemption (Ruth 4; Proverbs 31; Esther 6).

The Seven Maidens — Divine completeness and covenant provision (Genesis 1; Isaiah 11; Revelation 1).

The Crown and Favor — Humility exalted by divine providence (Luke 1:52; Philippians 2:6–7).

The Hidden Identity — Symbolic of divine concealment and timing (theme throughout Esther 2).

The Harem as Symbol — Contrast between human corruption and divine infiltration (Psalm 112:4).

The Reversal Motif — Echoed in 1 Corinthians 1:27 and fulfilled in Christ.

INTERLUDE: RETURN OF AMALEK

Primary Text

Genesis 3:15 — "I will put enmity between you and the woman, and between your seed and her seed; He shall bruise your head, and you shall bruise His heel."

— The foundational verse framing the cosmic conflict between the seed of the woman (Messiah) and the seed of the serpent.

Exodus 17:8–16 — The first appearance of Amalek and God's decree of perpetual war "from generation to generation."

Deuteronomy 25:17–19 — The command to remember Amalek's cruelty and the divine mandate to blot out his remembrance.

1 Samuel 15:1–35 — Saul's disobedience in sparing Agag and the incomplete fulfillment of divine judgment.

Esther 2:5; 3:1 — The genealogical link between Mordecai (descendant of Kish) and Haman (descendant of Agag), signaling the revival of the ancient conflict.

Thematic and Cross-References

Genesis 6:1–9 — The corruption of creation through the "sons of God" and the Nephilim; the beginning of spiritual defilement.

Genesis 14:5–7 — Abraham's battle against the coalition of eastern kings, including lands associated with the Rephaim and Amalekites.

Deuteronomy 3:11–13 — Og, king of Bashan, as the last of the Rephaim; a foreshadowing of spiritual strongholds later confronted by Christ.

1 Samuel 30:1–20; 2 Samuel 1:1–16 — David's battles with Amalek; physical conquest as a symbol of divine justice.

Psalm 68:21–22 — "God will strike the heads of His enemies... that your foot may crush them in blood." Echoes the Genesis 3:15 promise of ultimate victory.

Matthew 12:29 — "How can one enter a strong man's house and plunder his goods unless he first binds the strong man?" A metaphor for Christ's spiritual conquest.

Matthew 16:18 — Christ's declaration at Caesarea Philippi: "On this rock I will build My church, and the gates of Hades shall not prevail against it."

Mark 5:1–20 — The deliverance of the Gerasene demoniac in the region of the Decapolis—formerly the territory of Bashan.

Luke 10:19 — "Behold, I give you authority... over all the power of the enemy." Christ's commissioning of believers in covenant authority.

John 1:1–5 — The Word made flesh—the divine logos reclaiming the creation corrupted in Genesis 6.

Romans 8:37–39 — "In all these things we are more than conquerors through Him who loved us."

Ephesians 6:10–12 — "For we wrestle not against flesh and blood..." defining the ongoing war in the heavenly realm.

Colossians 2:15 — "He disarmed principalities and powers... triumphing over them by the cross."

1 Peter 3:19–22 — Christ's descent to proclaim victory to the imprisoned spirits; the fulfillment of divine justice.

Revelation 12:7–11 — The war in heaven and the ultimate defeat of the accuser "by the blood of the Lamb and the word of their testimony."

Doctrinal and Literary Allusions

The War of the Seeds — The perpetual conflict between covenant and corruption (Genesis 3:15).

The Amalekite Archetype — Embodiment of rebellion and divine opposition (Exodus 17; Deuteronomy 25).

The Nephilim and Rephaim Traditions — Representation of pre-Flood corruption and post-Flood defiance (Genesis 6; Deuteronomy 3).

Typology of Deliverers — Joshua, David, and Christ as progressive fulfillments of divine conquest (1 Samuel 17; Matthew 12:29).

Christ's Descent and Triumph — The harrowing of hell and victory proclamation (1 Peter 3:19–22; Colossians 2:15).

Spiritual Continuum — The Church's participation in ongoing covenant warfare through intercession and faith (Ephesians 6:10–18).

Ultimate Resolution — The serpent crushed, the covenant fulfilled, and the Bride empowered (Revelation 12:11; Romans 8:37–39).

CHAPTER THREE

Primary Text

Esther 3:1–15 — The elevation of Haman, Mordecai's refusal to bow, the casting of lots (Pur), and the issuing of the decree of destruction.

Thematic and Cross-References

Genesis 3:15 — "I will put enmity between you and the woman, and between your seed and her seed."

— Establishes the foundational conflict between the seed of the serpent and the seed of promise, echoed in the hostility between Haman and Mordecai.

Exodus 12:1–14 — Institution of the Passover.

258

— Parallels the irony of Haman's decree being written on the eve of Passover, symbolizing deliverance over-shadowing destruction.

Proverbs 16:33 — "The lot is cast into the lap, but its every decision is from the Lord."

— Central theological key to the chapter; God's sovereignty governs even the casting of Pur by Haman.

Acts 5:29 — "We must obey God rather than men."

— Reflects Mordecai's defiance before Haman and his allegiance to covenant loyalty over imperial command.

Genesis 50:20 — "You meant evil against me, but God meant it for good."

— The ultimate summary of divine reversal: Haman's decree of death becomes God's decree of deliverance.

1 Samuel 15:1–9, 32–33 — Saul's failure to destroy Agag.

— Establishes the historical and spiritual backdrop of unfinished conflict that now culminates through Mordecai's obedience.

Proverbs 3:6 — "In all your ways acknowledge Him, and He will direct your paths."

— Illustrates God's direction overruling human schemes, as seen in the providential "delay" of the decree.

Jonah 1:7 — Casting lots to reveal guilt.

— Another biblical instance where God's hand governs the outcome of casting, aligning with His divine justice.

Joshua 18:6–10 — Casting lots to divide the land.

— Demonstrates that lots, when used in covenant context, signify submission to God's will rather than chance.

Leviticus 16:8–10 — Casting lots for the scapegoat on the Day of Atonement.

— Symbolic of separation between guilt and grace, mirrored in Esther's theme of deliverance from judgment.

Acts 1:24–26 — The final casting of lots before Pentecost.

— Marks the transition from physical tokens of divine decision to spiritual guidance by the Holy Spirit.

Exodus 17:16 — "The Lord will have war with Amalek from generation to generation."

— Frames Haman's hatred as the reemergence of Amalek's ancient enmity against the covenant people.

Matthew 26:14–16 — Judas' betrayal for thirty pieces of silver.

— Foreshadows the parallel between Haman's pur-chase of death and Judas' purchase of betrayal.

Doctrinal and Literary Allusions

Acts 5:29 — "We must obey God rather than men."

— Illustrates Mordecai's covenant allegiance above earthly authority.

Proverbs 16:33 — God's sovereignty over the casting of lots (Pur), displaying providence even through pagan ritual.

Genesis 50:20 — The divine reversal motif—evil repurposed into redemption.

Proverbs 13:22 — "The wealth of the sinner is stored up for the righteous."

— Foreshadows Haman's estate becoming Mordecai's inheritance.

1 Peter 1:18–19 — The true currency of redemption—Christ's incorruptible blood contrasted with Haman's silver.

CHAPTER FOUR

Primary Text

Esther 4:1–17 — Mordecai's lament, Esther's awakening, the royal hesitation, and the commissioning through fasting and obedience.

Thematic and Cross-References

Psalm 34:18 — "The Lord is near to the brokenhearted and saves those who are crushed in spirit."

— Central to the theology of lament, illustrating God's nearness through grief and intercession.

Job 1:20–22 — Job's act of tearing his robe and worshiping through loss.

— Parallels Mordecai's posture of mourning as wor-ship rather than despair.

Jonah 3:5–10 — The repentance of Nineveh through fasting and sackcloth.

— Reflects the power of corporate repentance to invite divine mercy.

1 Samuel 1:10–11 — Hannah's weeping and vow before the Lord.

— Connects lamentation with prophetic intercession and birth of deliverance.

Romans 8:26 — "For the Spirit Himself intercedes for us with groanings too deep for words."

— Mirrors Hathach's role as intermediary and symbolizes the Holy Spirit's ministry of intercession.

Isaiah 49:15–16 — "Can a woman forget her nursing child?... I will not forget you. Behold, I have engraved you on the palms of My hands."

— Contrasts the silence of the Persian throne with the faithfulness of the heavenly one.

Daniel 3:18 — "But if not, we will not bow."

— Parallel of courageous surrender reflected in Esther's declaration, "If I perish, I perish."

Luke 22:42 — "Not My will, but Yours be done."

— Foreshadows the Christlike surrender of Esther's intercession through fasting.

Joel 2:12–14 — "Return to Me with all your heart, with fasting and weeping and mourning... Who knows if He will turn and relent?"

— Echoed in Mordecai's "Who knows" statement, blending faith with reverent humility.

2 Samuel 12:22 — "Who knows whether the Lord will be gracious to me?"

— The same idiom of divine mystery expressed through Mordecai's words to Esther.

Genesis 41:46; 2 Samuel 5:4; Luke 3:23

— Each marks "thirty" as a number of transition and commissioning, reflecting Esther's thirty-day waiting period before her pivotal act of obedience.

Isaiah 58:6 — "Is not this the fast that I have chosen: to loose the bonds of wickedness...?"

— Reveals fasting as spiritual warfare and divine intervention, not ritual.

Esther 4:16 — "If I perish, I perish."

— The climactic expression of surrender that transitions Esther from silence to calling.

Doctrinal and Literary Allusions

Psalm 51:17 — "A broken and contrite heart, O God, You will not despise."

— Illustrates lament as true worship and repentance as the foundation of intimacy.

Romans 12:1 — "Present your bodies as a living sacrifice, holy and acceptable to God."

— Reflects Esther's willingness to offer herself in obedience, merging priestly intercession with personal surrender.

Matthew 16:25 — "Whoever loses his life for My sake will find it."

— The spiritual principle embodied in Esther's self-offering for her people.

Hebrews 4:16 — "Let us then approach the throne of grace with confidence."

— The ultimate fulfillment of Esther's act—approaching the throne on behalf of others through faith, not fear.

CHAPTER FIVE

Primary Text

Esther 5:1–14 — Esther's approach before the king, the extension of the golden scepter, the first banquet with Ha-man, and the birth of Haman's prideful downfall.

Thematic and Cross-References

1 Kings 19:11–12 — "The Lord was not in the wind... but in a still small voice."

— Parallels Esther's post-fast silence, showing that divine guidance often comes through stillness rather than spectacle.

Hebrews 4:16 — "Let us therefore come boldly to the throne of grace..."

— Mirrors Esther's trembling approach to the throne as a type of the believer's access to God through Christ.

Ephesians 1:8 — "He lavished grace upon us."

— Reflects the king's extravagant favor as a shadow of God's abundant grace toward His people.

Ephesians 3:20 — "Now to Him who is able to do immeasurably more than all we ask or imagine..."

— Illustrates the exceeding generosity extended to Esther, foreshadowing divine overabundance through faith.

Mark 6:47–50 — Jesus walking on the storm.

— Symbolic parallel to faith rising in the middle of fear; grace meeting obedience "in the midst" of uncertainty.

Exodus 14:14 — "The Lord will fight for you; you need only to be still."

— Echoes Esther's restraint and divine timing as she waits for the right moment to reveal her request.

Psalm 23:5 — "You prepare a table before me in the presence of my enemies."

— The first banquet scene embodies divine irony—favor and danger coexisting under God's sovereignty.

Judges 6:12–15 — Gideon's fear and God's call.

— Reflects Esther's trembling obedience, showing that courage is forged through divine reassurance, not absence of fear.

2 Corinthians 12:9 — "My grace is sufficient for you, for My power is made perfect in weakness."

— Captures the essence of Esther's courage through weakness and dependence upon divine strength.

Proverbs 28:1 — "The wicked flee when no one pursues, but the righteous are bold as a lion."

— Parallels Mordecai's stillness at the gate as an image of holy boldness in quiet defiance.

Isaiah 48:22 — "There is no peace... for the wicked."

— Describes the unrest consuming Haman as pride corrodes his joy.

Psalm 73:18–19 — "Surely You set them in slippery places; You cast them down to destruction."

— Foretells the impending collapse of Haman's pride, born from false prosperity.

Matthew 10:28 — "Do not fear those who kill the body but cannot kill the soul..."

— Embodies Mordecai's spiritual composure rooted in reverent fear of God above man.

Doctrinal and Literary Allusions

Hebrews 11:6 — "Without faith it is impossible to please God."

— Underscores the theological centerpiece of Esther 5 as the turning point where faith activates divine reversal.

Romans 8:28 — "All things work together for good to those who love God..."

— Illustrates the providential pattern where Esther's waiting, the king's favor, and even Haman's plotting align toward redemption.

Psalm 75:6–7 — "For promotion comes neither from the east, nor from the west... but God is the Judge."

— Anticipates the reversal theme soon to manifest in Chapter 6 through divine exaltation and downfall.

Galatians 6:7 — "Whatever a man sows, that he will also reap."

— Foreshadows the spiritual justice of Haman's gallows— what he builds for another becomes his own snare.

1 Peter 5:5–6 — "God resists the proud but gives grace to the humble."

— Concludes the doctrinal contrast between Esther's humility and Haman's arrogance, framing the theological climax of Chapter 5.

CHAPTER SIX

Primary Text

Esther 6:1–14 — The sleepless king recalls Mordecai's past loyalty, Haman arrives to request his execution, and divine reversal unfolds as the proud man becomes the herald of the humble.

Thematic and Cross-References

Genesis 50:20 — "You meant evil against me, but God meant it for good."

— Captures the heart of Esther 6, where Haman's plot becomes the very means of Mordecai's exaltation.

Psalm 2:1–4 — "The nations rage... He who sits in the heavens laughs."

— Reflects God's sovereignty over human schemes and mirrors the irony of the sleepless king versus the restless enemy.

Psalm 121:4 — "He who keeps Israel neither slumbers nor sleeps."

— Connects to the sleepless king as a human shadow of the divine Watcher who never ceases to guard His people.

Malachi 3:16 — "A book of remembrance was written before Him for those who feared the Lord."

— Parallels the earthly chronicles read before Ahasuerus with God's heavenly "Book of Remembrance."

Romans 4:3 — "Abraham believed God, and it was credited to him as righteousness."

— Illustrates the principle of remembered faith and divine acknowledgment, echoed in Mordecai's delayed honor.

Habakkuk 2:3 — "The vision is yet for an appointed time... though it tarry, wait for it."

— Frames the timing of Mordecai's reward as deliberate, not delayed—God's precision in divine reversal.

Proverbs 16:9 — "A man's heart plans his way, but the Lord directs his steps."

— Describes the unseen orchestration of both the king's insomnia and Haman's arrival at dawn.

Proverbs 16:18 — "Pride goes before destruction, and a haughty spirit before a fall."

— The central moral principle embodied in Haman's downfall.

Psalm 37:12–13 — "The wicked plots against the righteous... but the Lord laughs at him."

— A direct commentary on the irony of Haman's plotting and God's timing of reversal.

Luke 14:11 — "Everyone who exalts himself will be humbled, and he who humbles himself will be exalted."

— Fulfilled in the chapter's reversal between Haman's humiliation and Mordecai's exaltation.

Philippians 2:8–9 — "He humbled Himself... therefore God highly exalted Him."

— Mirrors the Christological pattern of honor following humility, typified in Mordecai's elevation.

Isaiah 61:10 — "He has clothed me with the garments of salvation... the robe of righteousness."

— Symbolized through Mordecai being robed in royal garments.

Zechariah 9:9 — "Behold, your King is coming to you... humble and riding on a donkey."

— A prophetic foreshadowing of Christ's humble exaltation mirrored through Mordecai's procession.

Matthew 3:17 — "This is My beloved Son, in whom I am well pleased."

— Echoed in the declaration: "This is the man whom the king delights to honor."

Romans 8:1 — "There is therefore now no condemnation for those who are in Christ Jesus."

— Embodied in Mordecai's unexpected deliverance, where fear of judgment turns into honor.

John 3:17 — "For God did not send His Son into the world to condemn the world..."

— Parallels God's redemptive justice transforming judgment into mercy.

Romans 8:30 — "Those He justified, He also glorified."

— Expressed through Mordecai's transition from forgotten servant to exalted ruler.

2 Corinthians 7:10 — "Godly sorrow produces repentance... but worldly sorrow produces death."

— Contrasts Mordecai's grief of intercession with Haman's self-centered mourning.

Psalm 7:15–16 — "He who digs a pit will fall into it."

— Poetic justice fulfilled as Haman's schemes become the trap of his own downfall.

1 Corinthians 3:19 — "The wisdom of this world is foolishness with God."

— Applies to Haman's so-called "wise men," whose counsel dissolves into fatal irony.

Doctrinal and Literary Allusions

Romans 8:28 — "All things work together for good to those who love God."

— The defining theological axis of the chapter—providence weaving both good and evil intentions toward divine purpose.

Philippians 2:10–11 — "At the name of Jesus every knee should bow..."

— Foreshadowed in Haman, the unwilling herald of Mordecai's honor, symbolizing all creation bowing to Christ's glory.

Psalm 75:6–7 — "For exaltation comes neither from the east nor from the west... but God is the Judge."

— Captures the unseen hand behind Mordecai's elevation and Haman's fall.

Proverbs 21:30 — "There is no wisdom, nor understanding, nor counsel against the Lord."

— Summarizes the futility of Haman's advisors and the supremacy of divine counsel.

Revelation 18:9–10 — The fall of Babylon lamented by kings and merchants.

— Typologically reflected in Zeresh and Haman's "wise men," who now stand afar and mourn his ruin.

Psalm 1:1 — "Blessed is the man who does not walk in the counsel of the wicked."

— Concludes the moral thread of Chapter 6, contrasting Mordecai's faithfulness with Haman's fatal alliances.

CHAPTER SEVEN

Primary Text

Esther 7:1–10 — The king and Haman attend the banquet prepared by Queen Esther. She unveils Haman's plot, the king's wrath ignites, and the accuser is executed upon the very gallows he built.

Thematic and Cross-References

Esther 5:2 — The king extended the golden scepter to Esther.

— Foreshadows that her intercession in chapter seven flows from favor already received, not from fear of rejection.

Revelation 12:10–11 — "The accuser of our brothers... has been cast down... and they overcame him by the blood of the Lamb."

— Parallels the silencing of Haman (the accuser) before the king's throne with Satan's ultimate defeat before God's.

Hebrews 7:25 — "He ever lives to make intercession for them."

— Esther's plea before the king prefigures Christ's continual intercession for His people.

Romans 8:1 — "There is therefore now no condemnation for those who are in Christ Jesus."

— Reflects Esther's standing before the throne under favor, not judgment—symbolizing the believer's justification in grace.

Romans 8:33–34 — "Who shall bring a charge against God's elect? It is God who justifies."

— Mirrors the king's question: "Who is he that dares presume in his heart to do so?"—a divine rebuke to every accuser.

Ephesians 5:25–27 — "Christ loved the church and gave Himself for her... that He might present her to Himself in splendor."

— The king's defense of Esther mirrors the covenantal love of Christ defending His Bride.

Zechariah 2:8 — "He who touches you touches the apple of His eye."

— Echoes the king's fury at Haman's attempt to harm Esther, a type of divine jealousy for God's people.

Isaiah 54:17 — "No weapon formed against you shall prosper."

— Captures the futility of Haman's schemes as they collapse under divine protection.

John 10:10 — "The thief comes only to steal, kill, and destroy; I came that they may have life."

— Contrasts the decree of death Haman sought to enforce with the life and preservation granted through Esther's intercession.

Proverbs 29:23 — "A man's pride shall bring him low, but honor shall uphold the humble in spirit."

— Describes Haman's fall and Esther's rise—the moral axis of this chapter.

Proverbs 16:18 — "Pride goes before destruction, and a haughty spirit before a fall."

— The central spiritual law fulfilled in Haman's downfall.

Psalm 7:15–16 — "He made a pit and dug it out, and has fallen into the ditch which he made."

— A perfect summary of poetic justice as Haman dies upon his own gallows.

Exodus 17:14 — "I will utterly blot out the remembrance of Amalek from under heaven."

— Finds covenant fulfillment in Haman's death, erasing the Amalekite threat to God's people.

Deuteronomy 29:20 — "The LORD will blot out his name from under heaven."

— The covering of Haman's face symbolizes this ultimate erasure from remembrance.

Psalm 69:28 — "Let them be blotted out of the book of the living."

— Spiritually mirrors Haman's removal from covenant history.

Deuteronomy 4:24 — "The LORD your God is a consuming fire, a jealous God."

— Reflects the king's wrath as an earthly image of divine jealousy defending His covenant bride.

Isaiah 62:1 — "For Zion's sake I will not keep silent."

— Parallels Esther's decision to break her silence and intercede for her people.

John 16:8–11 — "He will convict the world concerning sin and righteousness and judgment."

— Reflected in Harbona's threefold witness: exposing sin (Haman's gallows), affirming righteousness (Mordecai's loyalty), and declaring judgment (execution).

Luke 12:2–3 — "Nothing is covered up that will not be revealed."

— Captures the moment Harbona reveals Haman's hidden plot before the king.

Isaiah 56:4–5 — "To the eunuchs... I will give within My temple a name better than sons and daughters."

— Prefigures Harbona's lasting remembrance as a faithful witness before the throne.

Romans 5:2 — "Through Him we have obtained access by faith into this grace in which we stand."

— Contrasts Esther's covenant access with Haman's revoked privilege—favor received versus favor forfeited.

Revelation 19:2 — "True and righteous are His judgments, for He has avenged the blood of His servants."

— Parallels the king's judgment as the manifestation of divine justice avenging covenant betrayal.

Revelation 20:10 — "The devil... was thrown into the lake of fire."

— Typologically fulfilled in Haman's destruction—the final fate of every accuser.

Psalm 75:6–7 — "For exaltation comes neither from the east nor the west... but God is the Judge."

— Underlines that reversal and justice come only from divine authority, not human effort.

Genesis 50:20 — "You meant evil against me, but God meant it for good."

— The governing principle of Esther's entire narrative, culminating in the downfall of evil through its own schemes.

Doctrinal and Literary Allusions

Romans 12:19 — "Vengeance is Mine; I will repay, says the Lord."

— Summarizes the divine justice seen in Haman's end.

2 Corinthians 3:18 — "We all, with unveiled face, beholding the glory of the Lord..."

— Contrasts Esther's unveiled access to the king with Haman's veiled condemnation.

Philippians 2:10–11 — "At the name of Jesus every knee should bow."

— Foreshadows the ultimate submission of all powers— just as Haman, the proud, is brought low before the King's decree.

Psalm 37:35–36 — "I have seen the wicked in great power... yet he passed away, and lo, he was not."

— Captures the swift disappearance of Haman's influence and the restoration of peace.

Esther 7:10 — "Then the king's wrath was pacified."

— Echoes covenant rest after judgment, much like the floodwaters subsiding (Genesis 8:1) or the cross bringing peace (Colossians 1:20).

CHAPTER EIGHT

Primary Text

Esther 8:1–17 — Esther receives Haman's house and entrusts it to Mordecai. A new decree is written, sealed with the king's ring, and sent to every province, granting the Jews authority to defend themselves. Mourning turns to joy, and many from other nations align themselves with God's people.

Thematic and Cross-References

Genesis 3:24 — "So He drove out the man..."

— The casting out of Haman from the king's presence parallels the first exile from God's presence, symbolizing judgment and separation from life.

Philippians 2:6–8 — Christ, though equal with God, humbled Himself.

— Esther's descent from royal elevation to intercession mirrors the humility of Christ's authority expressed through surrender.

Romans 8:17 — "Heirs of God, and joint-heirs with Christ."

— Esther's inheritance of Haman's estate and delegation to Mordecai prefigures the believer's shared inheritance in Christ's victory.

Ephesians 4:7–12 — "When He ascended on high... He gave gifts to men."

— Reflects the transfer of authority and spiritual gifts following victory, as Esther's favor flows through Mordecai to bless others.

Hebrews 7:25 — "He ever lives to make intercession for them."

— Esther's continued pleading before the king prefigures Christ's ongoing intercession for the redeemed.

Romans 8:2 — "For the law of the Spirit of life in Christ Jesus has set you free from the law of sin and death."

— The second decree of life superseding the first decree of death reveals the redemptive pattern of divine justice fulfilled through grace.

Matthew 5:17 — "I did not come to abolish the Law but to fulfill it."

— God's justice remains intact even as His mercy is revealed, echoed in the coexistence of the two royal decrees.

Ephesians 1:13–14 — "You were sealed with the promised Holy Spirit."

— The king's signet seal upon the decree typifies the Spirit's seal of ownership and permanence upon believers.

Acts 2:5–6 — "Every nation under heaven heard them in their own tongue."

— The sending of the decree to every province and language mirrors the Pentecostal sending of the Gospel to all nations.

Isaiah 55:11 — "My word... shall accomplish what I please."

— The decree sent in haste reflects the unstoppable nature of the King's word fulfilling divine purpose.

Exodus 12:36 — "They plundered the Egyptians."

— The Jews' right to plunder their attackers recalls Israel's redemption from Egypt and the reversal of oppression.

Proverbs 13:22 — "The wealth of the sinner is stored up for the righteous."

— The inheritance of Haman's estate by Esther fulfills this covenant principle of divine exchange.

Luke 11:21–22 — "When one stronger attacks... he divides the spoil."

— Christ's triumph over the strong man parallels the Jews' empowerment to stand against their enemies.

Ephesians 6:10–13 — "Put on the whole armor of God... to stand."

— The Jews' divine authorization to stand and defend themselves represents the believer's call to spiritual warfare through divine strength.

Isaiah 61:10 — "He has clothed me with the garments of salvation."

— Mordecai's royal robe and crown signify imputed righteousness and restored covenant relationship.

Colossians 3:4 — "When Christ... appears, you also will appear with Him in glory."

— Mordecai's emergence from obscurity into honor foreshadows the believer's future revelation in glory.

Psalm 30:11 — "You turned my mourning into dancing."

— The transformation of mourning in Susa into joy and celebration reflects redemptive reversal and restored fellowship.

Zechariah 8:23 — "Ten men... will take hold of one Jew's robe, saying, 'Let us go with you.'"

— The Persians who professed to be Jews signify nations drawn to covenant favor.

Isaiah 60:3 — "Nations shall come to your light."

— The nations' attraction to the visible blessing of God's people fulfills prophetic imagery of divine radiance revealed through redemption.

Romans 11:17–18 — "You... have been grafted in among the others."

— Foreshadows Gentile inclusion in covenant blessing as outsiders join under the decree of life.

Acts 5:11 — "Great fear came upon all who heard."

— The awe that fell on the nations mirrors holy reverence leading to repentance and alignment with divine authority.

Romans 8:37 — "In all these things we are more than conquerors through Him who loved us."

— Captures the believer's shared triumph under divine decree, moving from deliverance to dominion.

Doctrinal and Literary Allusions

Psalm 85:10 — "Mercy and truth have met together; righteousness and peace have kissed."

— Represents the convergence of law and grace through the two decrees.

1 Timothy 2:5 — "There is one God and one Mediator between God and men."

— Christ fulfills the mediatorial pattern that Esther could only prefigure.

Romans 5:2 — "Through Him we have access by faith into this grace in which we stand."

— The new decree parallels spiritual access and standing through grace.

Revelation 12:11 — "They overcame him by the blood of the Lamb."

— The Jews' authority to prevail mirrors the Church's spiritual victory through Christ's finished work.

Isaiah 61:3 — "To bestow on them a crown of beauty instead of ashes."

— The shift from lamentation to joy in Susa encapsulates divine restoration.

Luke 24:52–53 — "They returned to Jerusalem with great joy."

— The overflowing joy of the redeemed mirrors the rejoicing of Susa under the decree of life.

CHAPTER NINE

Primary Text

Esther 9:1–32 — The decree is fulfilled, the Jews gain victory over their enemies, the ten sons of Haman are slain, and the Feast of Purim is instituted as a perpetual remembrance of divine reversal and covenant joy.

Thematic and Cross-References

Joshua 2:9–11 — "The fear of you has fallen upon us..."

— echoes the dread that falls upon the enemies of the Jews, linking Esther's deliverance to Israel's covenant victories.

Deuteronomy 11:25 — "No man shall be able to stand before you..."

— divine favor and the transference of holy dread upon the nations.

Ephesians 6:10–13 — "Be strong in the Lord and in the power of His might..."

— the decree of empowerment parallels the believer's authority in spiritual warfare.

James 2:17 — "Faith without works is dead."

— the Jews' movement from fear to action mirrors faith manifesting through obedience.

Genesis 3:15 — "I will put enmity between you and the woman..."

— frames the hostility between Haman's house and God's covenant people as part of the ancient war of the seeds.

Exodus 17:14 — "I will utterly blot out the remembrance of Amalek from under heaven."

— fulfilled through the destruction of Haman's lineage and the judgment of his ten sons.

Genesis 14:23 — Abram's refusal to take spoils from Sodom

— reflected in the Jews' restraint from plundering, showing victory without greed.

1 Samuel 15:3, 9, 19 — Saul's failure to annihilate Amalek — reversed through the faithfulness of Mordecai's generation.

Luke 19:26 — "To everyone who has, more will be given."

— Mordecai's increasing authority exemplifies the multiplication of entrusted stewardship.

Colossians 2:15 — "He made a public spectacle of them, triumphing over them." — Haman's ten sons displayed upon the gallows signify the visible defeat of rebellion.

Proverbs 16:18 — "Pride goes before destruction..."

— the moral axis of Haman's fall extends to his lineage.

Revelation 17:12–14 — "The ten kings... will make war with the Lamb..."

— typological parallel between Haman's ten sons and the fullness of worldly rebellion under the Antichrist system.

Hebrews 4:9–10 — "There remains therefore a rest for the people of God."

— the Jews' "rest" after warfare prefigures eschatological rest following redemption.

Psalm 30:11 — "You turned my mourning into dancing."

— thematic culmination of reversal through joy and celebration.

Nehemiah 8:10 — "Send portions to those for whom nothing is prepared."

— the ethical fruit of deliverance expressed through generosity in the Feast of Purim.

Acts 1:8 — "You shall be My witnesses... to the ends of the earth."

— the expansion of Purim from Susa to the provinces mirrors redemption spreading from center to nations.

Psalm 9:7–8 — "He shall judge the world in righteousness."

— the king's justice on behalf of his people reflects divine vindication.

Philippians 1:6 — "He who began a good work in you will perform it until the day of Jesus Christ."

— Esther's continued intercession and Mordecai's decree fulfill God's redemptive completion.

Revelation 15:2–3 — "They sang the song of Moses and of the Lamb."

— the transition from battle to song parallels Israel's rest after divine victory.

Doctrinal and Literary Allusions

Esther 9:1; Genesis 50:20; Romans 8:28

— What was decreed for destruction becomes deliverance; God's providence transforms evil intent into redemptive purpose.

Esther 9:7–10; Revelation 17:12–14

— A symbol of complete rebellion under judgment, foreshadowing the fall of the ten kings allied against the Lamb.

Esther 9:10, 15, 16; Genesis 14:23; 1 Samuel 15:3, 9

— Victory without greed reflects covenant obedience and restores what Saul's disobedience forfeited.

Esther 9:16–17; Hebrews 4:9–10; Revelation 15:2–3

— The already/not-yet fulfillment of redemption; partial rest now, complete rest in Christ.

Esther 9:20–28; Psalm 30:11; Nehemiah 8:10; Luke 22:19

— Covenant remembrance through joy; sorrow transformed into celebration, prefiguring the Lord's Supper.

Esther 9:32; 6:1; Malachi 3:16; Revelation 20:12

— "It was written in the book" signifies victory sealed in divine record; memory itself becomes a weapon against forgetfulness.

CHAPTER TEN

Primary Text

Esther 10:1–3 — The king's final decree, Mordecai's exaltation, and the preservation of remembrance.

Thematic and Cross-References

Genesis 1:31 — "God saw all that He had made, and it was very good."

— The story concludes as creation did—order restored and goodness reaffirmed after conflict.

Exodus 17:14–16 — "I will utterly blot out the remembrance of Amalek from under heaven."

— The final peace under Mordecai echoes the fulfillment of this covenant promise of victory over the Amalekite spirit.

Psalm 9:7–8 — "But the Lord shall endure forever; He has prepared His throne for judgment."

— The king's justice on earth mirrors the eternal justice of the heavenly throne.

Psalm 37:37 — "Mark the blameless man, and observe the upright; for the future of that man is peace."

— Mordecai's life exemplifies righteous remembrance and covenant peace.

Ecclesiastes 3:14 — "Whatever God does endures forever."

— Reflects the lasting nature of divine providence recorded at Esther's conclusion.

Isaiah 46:9–10 — "My counsel shall stand, and I will accomplish all My purpose."

— God's unseen sovereignty governs every event from exile to restoration.

Daniel 2:20–21 — "He changes times and seasons; He removes kings and sets up kings."

— Captures the theme of divine order restored through earthly governance.

Romans 8:28 — "All things work together for good to those who love God."

— Summarizes the entire redemptive arc of Esther as providence turns tragedy into triumph.

Romans 8:17 — "Heirs of God, and joint-heirs with Christ."

— Mordecai's inheritance of authority mirrors the believer's spiritual inheritance through Christ.

1 Corinthians 15:57 — "Thanks be to God, who gives us the victory through our Lord Jesus Christ."

— The victory of the Jews becomes a shadow of ultimate victory over death and sin.

2 Corinthians 4:18 — "For the things which are seen are temporary, but the things which are unseen are eternal."

— Concludes the theme of divine concealment and revelation that defines the entire book.

Philippians 2:9–11 — "God has highly exalted Him... that at the name of Jesus every knee should bow."

— Mordecai's exaltation typifies Christ's ultimate glorification after humble obedience.

Colossians 3:3–4 — "Your life is hidden with Christ in God... when Christ appears, you also will appear with Him in glory."

— Parallels Esther's hidden identity now brought to light in glory and rest.

Jeremiah 29:13 — "You will seek Me and find Me when you search for Me with all your heart."

— God's invitation to deeper pursuit through revelation and faith.

Revelation 5:12–13 — "Worthy is the Lamb who was slain... to Him who sits on the throne and to the Lamb be blessing and honor."

— The final exaltation of the righteous in Esther foreshadows the eternal reign of Christ.

Doctrinal and Literary Allusions

Psalm 103:19 — "The Lord has established His throne in heaven, and His kingdom rules over all."

— Esther's earthly peace mirrors the heavenly order of divine rule.

Romans 11:33 — "Oh, the depth of the riches both of the wisdom and knowledge of God!"

— The hidden wisdom of God's providence revealed through Esther's story.

Ephesians 1:10 — "To unite all things in Christ, things in heaven and things on earth."

— The book's conclusion anticipates the ultimate restoration of all creation under Christ's authority.

2 Timothy 4:8 — "There is laid up for me the crown of righteousness."

— The crowning of Mordecai prefigures the believer's reward in glory.

Revelation 12:10–11 — "The accuser of our brothers has been cast down... and they overcame him by the blood of the Lamb."

— The silencing of Haman's line is the narrative fulfillment of victory over the accuser.

Revelation 21:6–7 — "It is done... He who overcomes shall inherit all things."

— The final rest of God's people mirrors the eschatological promise of inheritance and completion.

REFERENCES AND FURTHER READING

CHAPTER ONE

Primary Biblical Text

The Holy Bible, Modern English Version (MEV). Lake Mary, FL: Passio, 2014.

— Primary translation used for Scripture quotations and devotional study.

The Holy Bible, King James Version (KJV) — Archaeological Study Bible. Grand Rapids, MI: Zondervan, 2005.

— Used for historical, cultural, and geographical context relating to the Persian Empire, Ahasuerus (Xerxes I), and the book of Esther.

Historical Context and Background

Herodotus. The Histories. Translated by George Rawlinson. (Primary historical source on the reign of Xerxes I and the Persian Empire's customs, wars, and court life.)

The KJV Archaeological Study Bible. Thomas Nelson, 2008. (Provides archaeological and cultural background for the Persian period and the events surrounding the book of Esther.)

The Holy Bible, Modern English Version (MEV). Lake Mary, FL: Passio, 2014.

— Primary translation used for Scripture quotations and devotional study.

CHAPTER TWO

Primary Biblical Text

The Holy Bible, Modern English Version (MEV). Lake Mary, FL: Passio, 2014.

— Primary translation used for Scripture quotations and devotional study.

The Holy Bible, King James Version (KJV) — Archaeological Study Bible. Grand Rapids, MI: Zondervan, 2005.

— Used for historical, cultural, and geographical context relating to the Persian Empire, Ahasuerus (Xerxes I), and the book of Esther.

Historical and Cultural Context

Herodotus. Histories. Translated by Aubrey de Sélincourt. Revised by John Marincola. London: Penguin Classics, 2003.

— Books 1.133, 3.159, and 7–9 provide cultural and historical context for Persian administration, harem customs, and the reign of Xerxes I.

Briant, Pierre. From Cyrus to Alexander: A History of the Persian Empire. Winona Lake, IN: Eisenbrauns, 2002.

— Comprehensive account of Achaemenid administration, imperial policy, and royal ideology.

Kuhrt, Amélie. The Persian Empire: A Corpus of Sources from the Achaemenid Period. London: Routledge, 2007.

— Compilation of inscriptions, decrees, and primary texts illuminating Persian governance and culture.

Llewellyn-Jones, Lloyd. King and Court in Ancient Persia, 559–331 BCE. Edinburgh: Edinburgh University Press, 2013.

— Explores Persian court life, royal protocol, and the symbolic role of queens and eunuchs.

Linguistic and Theological Studies

Freedman, David Noel, ed. Anchor Yale Bible Dictionary. Vol. 2, "Esther." New Haven: Yale University Press, 1992.

— Examines the etymology and theological nuance of Esther ("hidden") and Hadassah ("myrtle") within Hebrew tradition.

Brown, Francis; Driver, S. R.; Briggs, Charles A. The Brown-Driver-Briggs Hebrew and English Lexicon. Peabody, MA: Hendrickson, 1996.

— Source for Hebrew lexical insights concerning concealment, providence, and covenant language.

Suggested Further Reading

Matthews, Victor H. Manners and Customs of the Bible. Peabody, MA: Hendrickson, 1991.

— Excellent guide to Near Eastern customs, court etiquette, and civic structures relevant to the Esther narrative.

Plutarch. The Rise and Fall of Athens: Nine Greek Lives. Translated by Ian Scott-Kilvert. London: Penguin Classics, 1960.

— Provides classical Greek perspective on Xerxes' campaign against Greece and its cultural aftermath.

INTERLUDE: RETURN OF AMALEK

Primary Biblical Text

The Holy Bible, Modern English Version (MEV). Lake Mary, FL: Passio, 2014.

— Primary translation used for Scripture quotations and devotional study.

The Holy Bible, King James Version (KJV) — Archaeological Study Bible. Grand Rapids, MI: Zondervan, 2005.

— Used for archaeological, cultural, and theological background related to the Amalekite conflict, covenant warfare, and ancient Near Eastern cosmology.

Historical and Contextual Sources

Van Dorn, Douglas. Giants: Sons of the Gods.

— Primary interpretive influence for contextual background on ancient Near Eastern cosmology, the Genesis 6 rebellion, the Rephaim, and covenant warfare motifs.

Van Dorn, Douglas. Kingdoms Unveiled (Podcast).

— Episodes referenced:
  • "Demons: Spirits of the Giants?"
  • "Giant Clans in the Bible?"

— Provides theological continuity on the "war of the seeds" from Genesis through Esther and the unseen realm's activity across redemptive history.

Blurry Creatures Podcast. Episode 315: "Serpent Mound of Bashan."

— Referenced for contextual parallels concerning Bashan, the Rephaim, and New Testament geography surrounding Caesarea Philippi.

Briant, Pierre. From Cyrus to Alexander: A History of the Persian Empire. Winona Lake, IN: Eisenbrauns, 2002.

— Consulted for historical continuity regarding the Persian setting, cultural backdrop, and imperial context surrounding the Esther narrative.

Kuhrt, Amélie. The Persian Empire: A Corpus of Sources from the Achaemenid Period. London: Routledge, 2007.

— Source for historical framework and Achaemenid cultural environment within which the Esther narrative unfolds.

Ancient Near Eastern Warfare and Cultural Context

Supplementary details derived from general historical overviews of the Persian Empire, Canaanite occupation, and Rephaim geography, as discussed in scholarly summaries and archaeological compendiums (via KJV Archaeological Study Bible notes and appendices).

— Used to situate the narrative of Esther within the broader context of covenant warfare and ancient imperial cosmology.

Early Jewish and Church Tradition

Referenced interpretive background concerning the disembodied spirits of the Nephilim (Genesis 6) and their later association with demonic activity, as recognized in ancient Jewish and early Christian commentary (notably intertestamental and patristic literature, including 1 Enoch, Jubilees, and writings of early Church Fathers such as Justin Martyr and Irenaeus).

— Used to support theological continuity between Genesis 6, the Amalekite lineage, and the typology fulfilled through Christ.

CHAPTER THREE

Primary Biblical Text

The Holy Bible, Modern English Version (MEV). Lake Mary, FL: Passio, 2014.

— Primary translation used for Scripture quotations and devotional study.

The Holy Bible, King James Version (KJV) — Archaeological Study Bible. Grand Rapids, MI: Zondervan, 2005.

— Used for historical, cultural, and geographical context relating to Achaemenid Persia, Pur/Purim, and the Esther narrative.

Historical and Cultural Context

Herodotus. The Histories. Translated by Aubrey de Sélincourt; revised by John Marincola. London: Penguin Classics, 2003.

— Books 1.133, 3.159, and 7–9 provide context for Persian administration, royal revenues, court custom, and the reign of Xerxes I.

Briant, Pierre. From Cyrus to Alexander: A History of the Persian Empire. Winona Lake, IN: Eisenbrauns, 2002.

— Comprehensive account of Achaemenid bureaucracy, imperial policy, and royal ideology, including fiscal structures behind large tribute sums.

Kuhrt, Amélie. The Persian Empire: A Corpus of Sources from the Achaemenid Period. London: Routledge, 2007.

— Compilation of inscriptions, decrees, and administrative texts illuminating imperial edicts, seals, and provincial communication.

Llewellyn-Jones, Lloyd. King and Court in Ancient Persia, 559–331 BCE. Edinburgh: Edinburgh University Press, 2013.

— Court ritual, promotion, honors, and political theater behind royal decisions.

Olmstead, A. T. History of the Persian Empire. Chicago: University of Chicago Press, 1948.

— Classic narrative history for chronology, campaigns, and court dynamics.

Cook, J. M. The Persian Empire. London: J. M. Dent, 1983.

— Concise overview of Achaemenid structures, communications, and satrapal governance.

Religion, Divination, and "Pur" (Casting Lots)

Freedman, David Noel, ed. Anchor Yale Bible Dictionary. New Haven: Yale University Press, 1992.

— Entries "Pur, Purim" and "Esther" for the Akkadian puru ("lot"), Purim background, and cultic/ritual context.

Boyce, Mary. Zoroastrians: Their Religious Beliefs and Practices. London: Routledge, 2001 (orig. 1979).

— Persian religious milieu and divinatory assumptions in the Achaemenid world.

Walton, John H., et al., eds. Zondervan Illustrated Bible Backgrounds Commentary: Old Testament (Esther). Grand Rapids, MI: Zondervan, 2009.

— Cultural backdrop for Pur/Purim, royal scribes, and decree dissemination.

Calendar, Dating (Nisan/Adar), and Festival Timing

Sarna, Nahum M. The JPS Bible Commentary: Esther. Philadelphia: Jewish Publication Society, 1987.

— Notes on Nisan/Adar timing, the literary irony of Passover eve and decree issuance, and Purim formation.

Jobes, Karen H. Esther (NIV Application Commentary). Grand Rapids, MI: Zondervan, 1999.

— Narrative and theological import of the dating formulae and festival allusions.

Linguistic and Theological Studies

Brown, Francis; Driver, S. R.; Briggs, Charles A. The Brown-Driver-Briggs Hebrew and English Lexicon. Peabody, MA: Hendrickson, 1996.

— Hebrew lexical insights for terms related to "lot," decree, seal, and covenant language.

**Koehler, Ludwig; Baumgartner, Walter; Richardson, M. E. J. The Hebrew and Aramaic Lexicon of the Old Testament (HALOT). ** Leiden: Brill, 1994–2000.

— Lexical notes for pur, edict/seal vocabulary, and legal terminology.

Suggested Further Reading

Matthews, Victor H. Manners and Customs of the Bible. Peabody, MA: Hendrickson, 1991.

— Near Eastern customs, court etiquette, and civic structures relevant to Esther.

Stern, Sacha. Calendar and Community: A History of the Jewish Calendar, 2nd Century BCE–10th Century CE. Oxford: Oxford University Press, 2001.

— Broader calendar background situating Nisan/Adar and festival resonances in Jewish memory.

CHAPTER FOUR

Primary Biblical Text

The Holy Bible, Modern English Version (MEV). Lake Mary, FL: Passio, 2014.

— Primary translation used for Scripture quotations and devotion-al study.

The Holy Bible, King James Version (KJV) — Archaeological Study Bible. Grand Rapids, MI: Zondervan, 2005.

— Background notes on mourning customs (sackcloth/ashes), fasting, palace protocol at the gate, and Persian court context relevant to Esther 4.

Historical and Cultural Context

Freedman, David Noel, ed. Anchor Yale Bible Dictionary. New Haven: Yale University Press, 1992.

— Entries consulted: "Sackcloth," "Fast, Fasting," "Gate," "Eunuchs," and "Esther" for cultural and ritual context of public lament, fasting, and gate functions in the ANE.

Zondervan Illustrated Bible Backgrounds Commentary: Old Testament (Vol. Esther). Grand Rapids, MI: Zondervan, 2009.

— Context on royal gates, access restrictions (Esth 4:2), and public mourning practices across the empire.

Matthews, Victor H. Manners and Customs of the Bible. Peabody, MA: Hendrickson, 1991.

— Concise overview of ANE mourning rites, sackcloth/ashes symbolism, and city-gate judicial/social functions.

Linguistic and Lexical Aids

Brown, Francis; Driver, S. R.; Briggs, Charles A. The Brown-Driver-Briggs Hebrew and English Lexicon. Peabody, MA: Hendrick-son, 1996.

— Hebrew lexical notes for terms related to mourning, fasting, and gate terminology.

Koehler, Ludwig; Baumgartner, Walter; Richardson, M. E. J. The Hebrew and Aramaic Lexicon of the Old Testament (HALOT). Leiden: Brill, 1994–2000.

— Proper-name and lexical notes (e.g., Hathach) and related vocabulary.

CHAPTER FIVE

Primary Biblical Text

The Holy Bible, Modern English Version (MEV). Lake Mary, FL: Passio, 2014.

— Primary translation used for Scripture quotations and devotion-al study.

The Holy Bible, King James Version (KJV) — Archaeological Study Bible. Grand Rapids, MI: Zondervan, 2005.

— Historical/archaeological notes consulted for Persian court customs, royal audience etiquette, and background to Esther 5.

Historical and Cultural Context

Herodotus. The Histories. Translated by Aubrey de Sélincourt; revised by John Marincola. London: Penguin Classics, 2003.

— Classical witness for Achaemenid court ceremony, banqueting culture, and royal policy.

Briant, Pierre. From Cyrus to Alexander: A History of the Persian Empire. Winona Lake, IN: Eisenbrauns, 2002.

— Authoritative synthesis on Achaemenid administration and royal ideology relevant to approach protocols and decrees.

Kuhrt, Amélie. The Persian Empire: A Corpus of Sources from the Achaemenid Period. London: Routledge, 2007.

— Primary inscriptions and administrative texts providing context for royal audiences, edicts, and court practice.

Llewellyn-Jones, Lloyd. King and Court in Ancient Persia, 559–331 BCE. Edinburgh: Edinburgh University Press, 2013.

— Detailed study of palace space, royal approach, queenly protocol, and the symbolism of the scepter.

Root, Margaret Cool. The King and Kingship in Achaemenid Art: Essays on the Creation of an Iconography of Empire. Leiden: Brill, 1979.

— Iconographic background (throne room "audience scenes," scepter imagery, spatial staging) that illuminates Esther 5:1.

Yamauchi, Edwin M. Persia and the Bible. Grand Rapids, MI: Baker, 1990.

— Historical backdrop for Persian customs, audience rules, and material culture intersecting the Esther narrative.

Literary and Theological Studies

Sarna, Nahum M. The JPS Bible Commentary: Esther. Philadelphia: Jewish Publication Society, 1987.

— Notes on narrative structure, the rhetorical function of Esther's approach, and the banquet strategy.

Berlin, Adele. Esther: The Traditional Hebrew Text with the New JPS Translation. Philadelphia: Jewish Publication Society, 2001.

— Literary analysis of irony, reversal, and the central pivot of the book around Esther's initiative.

Fox, Michael V. Character and Ideology in the Book of Esther. 2nd ed. Grand Rapids, MI: Eerdmans, 2001.

— Discussion of plot architecture (including the central turning point), character motivation, and thematic reversal.

CHAPTER SIX

Primary Biblical Text

The Holy Bible, Modern English Version (MEV). Lake Mary, FL: Passio, 2014.

— Primary translation used for Scripture quotations and devotional study.

The Holy Bible, King James Version (KJV) — Archaeological Study Bible. Grand Rapids, MI: Zondervan, 2005.

— Used for historical/archaeological notes on Persian court practice, royal records, and honorific customs.

Historical & Cultural Context

Herodotus. Histories. Translated by Aubrey de Sélincourt; revised by John Marincola. London: Penguin Classics, 2003.

— Court protocol, royal favors, and administrative practice in the Achaemenid period (esp. Books 1, 3, 7–9).

Llewellyn-Jones, Lloyd. King and Court in Ancient Persia, 559–331 BCE. Edinburgh: Edinburgh University Press, 2013.

— Royal etiquette, inner-court access, public honors, and the political theater of exaltation.

Kuhrt, Amélie. The Persian Empire: A Corpus of Sources from the Achaemenid Period. London: Routledge, 2007.

— Primary inscriptions and administrative texts illuminating royal decrees, record-keeping, and ceremonial practice.

Briant, Pierre. From Cyrus to Alexander: A History of the Persian Empire. Winona Lake, IN: Eisenbrauns, 2002.

— Synthesis of Achaemenid governance, promotion, and imperial ideology relevant to Esther 6.

Olmstead, A. T. History of the Persian Empire. Chicago: University of Chicago Press, 1948.

— Classic narrative background for Xerxes' reign, court dynamics, and the broader historical setting.

Linguistic & Lexical Aids

Brown, Francis; Driver, S. R.; Briggs, Charles A. The Brown-Driver-Briggs Hebrew and English Lexicon. Peabody, MA: Hendrick-son, 1996.

— Lexical notes for sēfer ("book/scroll"), zikrōn ("remembrance/record"), and honorific terms.

Koehler, Ludwig; Baumgartner, Walter; Richardson, M. E. J. The Hebrew and Aramaic Lexicon of the Old Testament (HALOT). Leiden: Brill, 1994–2000.

— Entries for remembrance/record terminology and royal-ceremonial vocabulary in Esther 6.

Esther Scholarship & Narrative/Literary Analysis

Sarna, Nahum M. The JPS Bible Commentary: Esther. Philadelphia: Jewish Publication Society, 1987.

— Notes on royal insomnia, "book of chronicles," and reversal as a literary device.

Berlin, Adele. Esther: The JPS Commentary. Philadelphia: Jewish Publication Society, 2001.

— Narrative irony, timing, and the mechanics of reversal in Esther 6.

Jobes, Karen H. Esther (NIV Application Commentary). Grand Rapids, MI: Zondervan, 1999.

— Theological and literary reflections on remembrance, honor, and providence.

Fox, Michael V. Character and Ideology in the Book of Esther. 2nd ed. Grand Rapids, MI: Eerdmans, 2001.

— Analysis of characterization (king/Haman/Mordecai) and the ideology of exaltation/humiliation in the chapter.

Suggested Further Reading

Matthews, Victor H. *Manners and Customs of the Bible.* Peabody, MA: Hendrickson, 1991.

— Helpful cultural background on court gates, officials, and honor-shame dynamics that frame Esther 6.

CHAPTER SEVEN

Primary Biblical Text

The Holy Bible, Modern English Version (MEV). Lake Mary, FL: Passio, 2014.

— Primary translation for Scripture quotations and devotional study.

The Holy Bible, King James Version (KJV) — *Archaeological Study Bible.* Grand Rapids, MI: Zondervan, 2005.

— Notes consulted for historical, cultural, and legal background in Esther, including court protocol, eunuchs, and execution terminology ("gallows"/stake).

Historical & Cultural Context

Herodotus. *The Histories.* Trans. Aubrey de Sélincourt; rev. John Marincola. London: Penguin Classics, 2003.

— Core classical witness for Achaemenid court life, royal feasts, and Persian use of impalement as capital punishment (e.g., Darius), framing the scene of Esther 7.

Briant, Pierre. *From Cyrus to Alexander: A History of the Persian Empire.* Winona Lake, IN: Eisenbrauns, 2002.

— Authoritative synthesis on Achaemenid administration, royal ideology, punishments, and inner-court dynamics surrounding advisors/eunuchs.

Kuhrt, Amélie. The Persian Empire: A Corpus of Sources from the Achaemenid Period. London: Routledge, 2007.

— Primary inscriptions and administrative texts illuminating court procedure, decrees, and the mechanics of royal justice.

Llewellyn-Jones, Lloyd. King and Court in Ancient Persia, 559–331 BCE. Edinburgh: Edinburgh University Press, 2013.

— Court etiquette, audience protocols, and the role of eunuchs, helpful for reading Harbona's proximity to the throne in Esther 7.

Zondervan Illustrated Bible Backgrounds Commentary: Old Testament (Vol. Esther). Grand Rapids, MI: Zondervan, 2009.

— Clarifies "gallows" (Heb. ʿēṣ) as a stake/pole and situates the banquet-to-judgment movement within ANE legal culture.

Literary & Theological Studies

Berlin, Adele. Esther: The Traditional Hebrew Text with the New JPS Translation. Philadelphia: Jewish Publication Society, 2001.

— Analysis of courtroom imagery, naming conventions (e.g., Harbona), and the unraveling of Haman through narrative irony.

CHAPTER EIGHT

Primary Biblical Text

The Holy Bible, Modern English Version (MEV). Lake Mary, FL: Passio, 2014.

— Primary translation used for Scripture quotations and devotional study.

The Holy Bible, King James Version (KJV) — Archaeological Study Bible. Grand Rapids, MI: Zondervan, 2005.

— Consulted for cultural and historical context regarding Persian law, seals, royal decrees, and ancient Near Eastern administrative customs.

Historical and Cultural Context

Herodotus. The Histories. Translated by Aubrey de Sélincourt; revised by John Marincola. London: Penguin Classics, 2003.

— Describes Persian legal systems, royal messengers, the use of signet rings, and the process of issuing empire-wide decrees.

Briant, Pierre. From Cyrus to Alexander: A History of the Persian Empire. Winona Lake, IN: Eisenbrauns, 2002.

— Authoritative overview of Achaemenid governance, imperial communications, and administrative hierarchy within which Esther's decree operates.

Kuhrt, Amélie. The Persian Empire: A Corpus of Sources from the Achaemenid Period. London: Routledge, 2007.

— Provides primary source inscriptions and documentation on Persian law, courier systems, and official correspondence similar to those depicted in Esther 8.

Llewellyn-Jones, Lloyd. King and Court in Ancient Persia, 559–331 BCE. Edinburgh: Edinburgh University Press, 2013.

— Explores Persian court life, symbolism of royal garments, and the political theology behind the king's favor and decrees.

CHAPTER NINE

Primary Biblical Text

The Holy Bible, Modern English Version (MEV). Lake Mary, FL: Passio, 2014.

— Primary translation used for Scripture quotations and devotional study.

The Holy Bible, King James Version (KJV) — Archaeological Study Bible. Grand Rapids, MI: Zondervan, 2005.

— Consulted for historical, cultural, and theological background relating to the Persian Empire, covenant warfare typology, and post-decree context in Esther 9.

Historical and Cultural Context

Herodotus. The Histories. Translated by Aubrey de Sélincourt; revised by John Marincola. London: Penguin Classics, 2003.

— Primary classical source describing Persian administration, military customs, and execution practices, contextualizing Esther 9's imperial justice and public displays.

**Briant, Pierre. From Cyrus to Alexander: A History of the Persian Empire. ** Winona Lake, IN: Eisenbrauns, 2002.

— Comprehensive historical synthesis on Achaemenid gover-nance, legal decrees, and provincial responses to royal policy, illuminating the decree's fulfillment in Esther 9.

**Kuhrt, Amélie. The Persian Empire: A Corpus of Sources from the Achaemenid Period. ** London: Routledge, 2007.

— Compilation of inscriptions and administrative documents offering background for Persian decrees, record-keeping, and empire-wide enforcement of royal edicts.

**Llewellyn-Jones, Lloyd. King and Court in Ancient Persia, 559–331 BCE. ** Edinburgh: Edinburgh University Press, 2013.

— Details Persian court life, legal symbolism, and the dynamics of royal justice relevant to Haman's sons' execution and the celebration of Purim.

Linguistic, Theological, and Typological Studies

**Freedman, David Noel, ed. Anchor Yale Bible Dictionary. ** New Haven: Yale University Press, 1992.

— Entries "Amalek," "Purim," and "Esther" consulted for theological and lexical context regarding covenant warfare, judgment, and divine reversal.

**Brown, Francis; Driver, S. R.; Briggs, Charles A. The Brown-Driver-Briggs Hebrew and English Lexicon. ** Peabody, MA: Hendrick-son, 1996.

— Lexical source for Hebrew terminology related to "rest," "remember," "reverse," and "destroy," reinforcing the narrative's covenantal and moral vocabulary.

**Koehler, Ludwig; Baumgartner, Walter; Richardson, M. E. J. The Hebrew and Aramaic Lexicon of the Old Testament (HALOT). ** Leiden: Brill, 1994–2000.

— Consulted for lexical and etymological precision concerning decree, vengeance, and remembrance terminology in Esther 9.

Intertextual and Eschatological Parallels

**Van Dorn, Douglas. Giants: Sons of the Gods. ** Monument, CO: Waters of Creation, 2013.

— Background source for understanding biblical "seed war" motifs and their continuation through Amalekite lineage typology.

CHAPTER TEN

Primary Biblical Text

The Holy Bible, Modern English Version (MEV). Lake Mary, FL: Passio, 2014.

— Primary translation used for Scripture quotations and theological synthesis.

Historical and Cultural Context

Herodotus. The Histories. Translated by Aubrey de Sélincourt; revised by John Marincola. London: Penguin Classics, 2003.

— Background on Persian administrative policy, tribute systems, and the reign of Xerxes I.

Briant, Pierre. From Cyrus to Alexander: A History of the Persian Empire. Winona Lake, IN: Eisenbrauns, 2002.

— Comprehensive historical framework for Persian governance, tribute, and imperial restoration under Xerxes.

Kuhrt, Amélie. The Persian Empire: A Corpus of Sources from the Achaemenid Period. London: Routledge, 2007.

— Primary inscriptions and imperial decrees related to taxation, census, and empire administration.

ABOUT THE AUTHOR

Tabitha Min has always believed that stories—whether spoken or written—carry a wonder all their own, one that stays with the reader long after the final page is turned.

She lives in rural South Carolina with her husband and their children. When she's not caring for her family or tending to the home, Tabitha is often working on her next project, reading, or outlining new ideas for the stories ahead.

But her journey is far from over. To discover more about her work, her creations, and the stories yet to come, visit:

www.tabithamin.com

OTHER WORKS BY TABITHA MIN

HARU'S WORLD
CHILDREN'S BOOK (2024)

Haru, a little toadstool mush-room, comes to life when a sprinkle of magical dust falls from an ancient oak tree. Awakened to a world of wonder, Haru embarks on a journey of discovery, seeing everything through new eyes and making delightful friends along the way.

FENNEL'S LIGHT
CHILDREN'S BOOK (2025)

When Fennel, a small and unassuming creature, receives an ordinary candle from a wandering traveler, he thinks little of it—until he lights the wick and glimpses a distant glow on the horizon. Compelled by a force he cannot explain, Fennel leaves behind the only home he's ever known to follow the light.

Guided by the flickering glow, Fennel's journey is not without struggle. He faces temptation, deception, and a darkness that seeks to snuff out his flame. But through every trial, the light remains, beckoning him onward.

An allegorical fantasy tale reminiscent of Pilgrim's Progress, Fennel's Light is a stirring fable about perseverance, trust, and the faith to walk forward even when the path is uncertain.

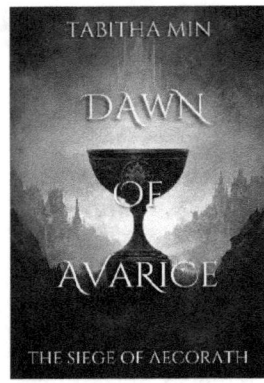

DAWN OF AVARICE
BOOK ONE (2023)

Ludica, king of Faermire, has devoted years to building a powerful legacy for his three children. But when the sudden death of a rival king stirs whis-pers of conflict across the land, Ludica realizes that threats to his reign are closer than he imagined—both beyond his borders and within them.

As Gwenora, the widowed queen, offers Ludica a treaty to secure peace, they both recognize that such an alliance risk inciting rebellion among their own people.

Meanwhile, Ludica's eldest children, Beowyn and Estrith, uncover a plot involving their uncle and stepmother, aimed at seizing the throne. Yet, in bringing the truth to light, they face consequences that threaten to unravel the world around them.

With treasonous alliances, deadly conspiracies, and fractured loyalties at every turn, Ludica and his family must rely on each other to hold their places in the kingdom of Aecorath—or risk losing everything they hold dear.

Scan the QR code to step beyond the page and immerse yourself in the animated audiobook of *Dawn of Avarice*. Watch the story unfold with captivating narration, rich sound design, and stunning visuals that bring the world of Aecorath to life.

PERDITION RISING
BOOK TWO (2025)

The realm teeters on the edge of chaos, and those who remain must navigate treachery, war, and forces beyond mortal understanding.

Beowyn never sought the crown, but with the throne thrust upon him, he must prove his worth—or risk losing everything. His sister, Estrith, will stop at nothing to save their brother, Siged, from a dark affliction—one that threatens not only his life but the very fabric of their king-dom.

Meanwhile, Sidonis, bound to a fate he does not fully comprehend, walks a dangerous path between ambition and the will of the gods.

Old enemies rise, new alliances take shape, and unseen forces stir beneath the surface. As Aecorath descends further into conflict, those at the center of it all must decide how much they are willing to sacrifice—for power, for loyalty, and for survival.

The gods are watching. The war has only begun.

Stay up to date with the latest projects, upcoming releases, and handcrafted creations. Whether it's new additions to the Siege of Aecorath series, exclusive artwork, or unique, story-inspired items from The Curious Emporium, there is always some-thing new on the horizon.

Explore current works, discover what's to come, and be the first to know about future adventures. Join the journey and step into a world where stories take shape beyond the page.

Books are available for purchase directly through the website or can be found on Amazon.com.

Visit to learn more

www.tabithamin.com